Not Normal Things

CATE MCMURRAY

This book is a memoir. It reflects the author's present recollections of experiences over time. Some sections of the narrative have been enhanced to improve the storyline.

ISBN: 978-1-913479-60-2 (paperback)
ISBN: 978-1-913479-61-9 (ebook)

www.thatguyshouse.com

In the pursuit of being normal, her soul grew tired and her eyes lost their sparkle. She couldn't find it, so she sought it even harder, and as she did her limbs grew weary and her voice became so quiet it was all but a whisper. But on her perilous quest to be like everyone else, and within the corners of every "Not Normal Thing" that she experienced as a result, she discovered that her own truth was the most normal thing in the world. And as she stepped into the familiarity of it, her eyes lit up, and her smile widened, until one day, she was so completely and weirdly Her, that her soul danced the dance of a thousand fireflies…

even when there was no music to be heard.

Introduction

Weird things have always happened to me. Weird things, at weird times. I spent a lot of my life wondering if things would ever be easy, and longing to be like every-one else. I *just* wanted to be normal but it never seemed to go that way, and then at the age of thirty-nine, everything changed. As all that I knew was stripped away from me, things finally started falling into place.

My second marriage was failing and had left me pretty much bereft. I had no money, nothing of any financial value, no home, no car, no job and worst of all, no confidence at all. I had isolated myself from my family, and the few friends who were left, so that none of them would know the secrets that I had been forced to carry for the couple of years previous.

I hated myself, I hated what I had become, and I hated my life. I woke up on November 11th 2013, and as I opened my eyes the only thought I could tolerate was the one that told me that I wanted to die. I remember lying in bed. It was early and as the sun shone through the curtains, all I could think was "I don't want to be here anymore". I assessed all the different options for how I could end my life. I thought about taking a ton of tablets, and assessed how many I had in the house. It became apparent that having a husband who's gambling addiction had brought everyone to their knees, also meant that even taking an overdose wasn't possible...when you are penniless with four children, buying ibuprofen, quite obviously, is not your main priority. My thoughts turned to the memory of the gun my dad used to keep in the top of his wardrobe underneath his jumpers; as a child I used to sneak in the bedroom sometimes and carefully pick it up. I remembered how heavy it was, and how the engraved pattern on its butt was almost sharp and hurt my soft palms. I remembered how when I held it I wasn't quite strong enough and the barrel end would fall forwards because of the unexpected weight. I'd manage it now. I was totally lost in dark thoughts about driving the car into trees, walls, anything sturdy enough that would hurt me but not harm anyone else, when one of my children shouted for me. The tears started coming at that point and soon turned into a full-blown sob as I realised that there was no way I could leave them. What was I doing? What was I thinking!? How could I think such things when my entire life was only a few steps away in another room? They were (are) everything to me, they needed me too, and I felt guilty and ashamed for even considering what I had been a few seconds before. Of course, it didn't change how I felt inside, but I knew I had to do *something*; so, I did.

Fast forward a few months and everything I thought I knew was turned on its head, and although I was still flailing around in the darkness, for the first time in a long time, life felt weirdly safe. I'd been through many traumas by this time in my life, but this was by far the biggest, darkest, most difficult thing I'd ever had to deal with. I had come to realise that when all aspects of your life feel wrong, in order for everything to fall into place, it first has to fall apart. It became clear that when you feel surrounded by darkness, the beauty of a single fraction of light is astonishing, but that light is not always gifted to us; sometimes we must create it for ourselves.

In the three years that followed, I found my own light switch, and amongst the giant ball of twine that I started to unravel, I discovered that all of the Not Normal Things I had experienced, had happened to me for good reason and at the perfect time too. I just hadn't seen them for what they really were, and I had used *all* the worst techniques for dealing with them (or not dealing with them whatsoever, as the case may be).

So, I started learning and submerged myself into a whole new world of knowledge and understanding. I viewed a million webinars, podcasts, interviews, YouTube videos... you name it, I watched it! I read hundreds of books on every wellbeing, spiritual, self-help topic you can imagine. Some I loved, some I didn't, and some changed the course of my life for good; it didn't matter, I consumed them all. I studied Witchcraft and the Occult in a way I never had before, and made huge decisions based on what I learnt. There was a driving force inside me, willing me on to figure out whatever it was that I knew was waiting for me, and my life started to look and feel very different.

After the dust had settled a little, it became abundantly clear to me that not being normal was in fact, my normal, and that all the Not Normal Things that happened to me were just the lessons that come to everyone wrapped up in a very "not normal" package because they had to be. I learnt that acknowledging and healing trauma is dark and dirty work (yes, WORK! Full on, balls deep, gritty, nasty work!) but is also totally worth every single second of the pain. It's not only worth it, but it's completely necessary if you want to affect any kind of lasting change in your life. The evolution of your soul can only happen once your heart has been cracked apart so badly that the pieces don't fit together like they used to anymore. That's what forces you to learn a new way of being, and once you've done that, nothing is ever the same again.

All of the leaders, gurus and coaches that I learned from spoke about awakening and enlightenment, and I wasn't sure what it really was. Would there be this flash of white light and some angels singing, before my crown burst open and the gift of enlightenment was bestowed upon me? I didn't know what to expect, and wasn't even sure I'd ever be "good enough" to earn such an award, but I brushed my curiosity aside and ploughed forwards. Some-time later, after years of constant submergence into all things esoteric and hours and hours of what I had determined to be my own spiritual practice, I realised that awakening can be felt, although it's not wrapped up in a shiny box with a clearly written label on. I realised that awakening is taking a deep breath when someone shouts or vents their anger at me for no good reason. It's smiling at someone in the supermarket just because I want to, and not being upset if they don't smile back. It's loving people more in their dark times without complaint or limitation, but with very real awareness about how much I have to give. It's about choosing what's good for my lifestyle and belief systems without judgement about anyone who isn't making the same choices. It's about being able to push past my ego and do what's in my soul without worrying what others think. It's about love; love for all things, at all times, in all spaces, including myself.

I'd be lying if I said I haven't since felt my crown blow wide open and felt that white light energy enter every fibre of my being on several occasions since then, but it was only when I let go of the expectation of what might be, and realised what was, that it happened.

And now, my soul calls me to write this book. I've been longing to do so for many years, so here she is. She's a collection of stories; heart-warming stories, bone chilling stories, sad stories and stories of triumph! She's more than that too though. She's a mirror to hold up to yourself, a candle to light the way, a toolkit of practical advice, a bible of spiritual takeaways, and a journey through the unknown into what is. She's for you, and me. She's for anyone who has ever wondered what the actual fuck is going on in their life and why weird, awful, difficult stuff always happens to them. She's for the ones who feel lost and don't know who the hell they are anymore, and probably never have known. She's for the ones who are currently navigating weirdness of their own and need some guidance, or maybe even hope. She's for the emotional, the over-givers, the silent ones. She's for anyone who wants to figure out their shit and wonders what's on the other side of it. She's here to help you see that even when you don't know the answer, *you know the answer*, and that you *can* bring about huge change for yourself and create a life you love!

My hope is that she will make you uncomfortable in your comfortableness, and reassure you that you are perfect as you are *right now*. The world needs you to be exactly who you were born to be, and within the pages of this book I hope you will find the magick that enables you to unlock any shackle that is keeping you from stepping into the brightest version of yourself.

Most of all, I hope she shows you that Not Normal Things are the key to happiness - the sort of happiness that right now, you might only think exists in fairy tale endings, but is absolutely yours for the taking if you're brave enough to truly face the twists and turns of your own story first.

Much Love,

Cate x

P.S.

On a side note...I'm a total Spirit Junkie and came out of the broom-closet some time ago, but that doesn't mean that I'm always right, or have it all figured out. Just like you, I'm a spiritual being having a very human experience, and with that, comes constant learning and growth. Anyone who tells you there is an end goal in Spirituality doesn't truly understand the ever-evolving nature that it is to be here on this plane, at this time. Of course, there are levels of learning and growth, and with every new level comes a new teacher, but it won't ever stop for any of us. As such, I can only tell you what I have learnt, and hope that it fits with the level that you're at right now as you're turning these pages.

Magick:

The science and art of causing change to occur in conformity to will, including mundane acts of will as well as ritual magick.

Magick is that which happens as a result of spiritual practice or acts of radical self-awareness.

Not Normal Things #1
Seeing & Hearing Dead People
Part I

My first experience of hearing and seeing spirit (that I can remember) happened when I was about five years old. Of course, I didn't know that's what it was then, and that's probably why I wasn't frightened either. As far as I was concerned, I just heard and felt people that didn't exist, and I think at that age I didn't really even question it; it was just something that happened.

It was subtle in the early days, an unexpected feeling of someone, or something, breathing in my ear when I was looking the other way. A voice I didn't recognise that was loud enough to make me turn around but not loud enough to be real.

The first time I remembered it happening it was fleeting and gentle, and took place in one of the bedrooms in our house, which was a home vastly different to most people's.

My parents had starting managing a snooker club when I was three. It was a live-in position, so we (my two sisters, my Mum and Dad and me) had moved into this grand, beautiful and vast Victorian building with the snooker room and bar on the top floor and the living quarters on the bottom, a couple of years previously. We wouldn't have understood it at the time, but as we got older, this wonderful place become a veritable playground for my two younger sisters and I. Our large bedroom was on the ground floor at the front, and it had the biggest windows I'd ever seen! It was a lovely room, and one that my sisters and I shared together.

One particular morning I'd woken and I was sat upright about to get out of bed. Out of nowhere, I felt a breeze sweep across my face, and at the same time I heard someone call my name.

"Catherine…"

It was the soft and rather beautiful voice of a woman, not one that I knew, and I could almost feel her hand lovingly stroke my cheek as the whisper disappeared into the ether.

Looking back, I don't really know what I thought about it at that stage of my life, but I do know that it didn't scare me, or confuse me enough to tell my Mum, and I guess I thought it happened to everyone. It wouldn't be long until that changed though, and very soon my experiences of spirit would become much more than whisperings or quiet breezes of air, and I would know what it felt like to feel very afraid of things that I couldn't explain.

There were two staircases in the club. One was part of the main entrance hall to the building that the general public used as the entry and exit to the snooker club, and a smaller one, just for us, which led directly from the living quarters to the door of the snooker room.

The main staircase was imposing with its incredibly wide steps and beautiful sweeping oak banister. There were about ten steps down

2

to a large landing before another, much longer, set of steps. The wide, always shiny, wooden banister swept down them all with the kind of grandeur that you would expect from a building that was enhanced in the 1870's, and in the years that we lived there, my sisters and I flew down it on our bottoms, squealing with excitement (and a little bit of fear) many, many times.

The smaller staircase was encased by stone walls and had a door at the top. It couldn't be more different from its sister staircase, and its small steps wound tightly around a corner before leading down to a second wooden door. When the door at the bottom was shut, the staircase was dark and whilst it may not have been very long, the trip down it felt uneasy and made the hairs on the back of my neck stand up, even if I was with someone else.

The snooker room was huge and housed two full size snooker tables, a few dart boards, and a stage for spectators to sit and watch the ongoing matches. There were little wooden benches like small church pews around the edges of the room. The windows were small and original to the building. They adorned both sides of the room, but not the back wall.

When it was busy it was filled with men (and the occasional woman) taking their sport seriously, and yet there was always laughter and a great feeling of comradery. I remember the blue chalk, the sound of the cues hitting the balls and the creaking of the ancient floorboards as people moved round the tables positioning themselves for their next shot. It was a fun place to be when we were allowed in, and the glass of coke and KitKat we always got, only added to the fun!

When it was empty, it was *very* different. It was cold, slightly foreboding and deathly quiet. There was a weird undercurrent of

3

energy that made me feel uneasy, and although I didn't understand why it made me so uncomfortable, I really didn't like it.

The first time I ever felt really frightened of something I couldn't actually see was in that room. I was about eight years old and I'd gone in there as my sisters and I were playing hide and seek. You might think that was a slightly odd place to choose to hide if you didn't like being in a room, but the legs of the snooker tables were as wide as tree-trunks, and I could get underneath the tables and hide perfectly behind them without being seen. It was, of course, one of our favourite hiding places, but with the house being so big, it was one of many.

The building was echoey, and you could easily hear the footsteps of people moving around. You could hear the pitter patter of shoes on the cold, hard, ancient flagstone floor that covered the dining room, and the same tell-tale sound also gave away any movement on the Minton tiled hallways and corridors – even those made by the quietest of tippy-toes. The smaller staircase would creak under the slightest weight, and there were so many doors that it was almost impossible to travel anywhere silently.

As I crouched behind the giant table leg of the first table in the room, I could hear my little sister making her way through the house on her mission to find one of us. I heard doors opening, and little shoes quietly running down the carpeted landing. From behind the table leg, I saw the door handle of the snooker room depress, and it opened slowly. Just as I expected her to enter the room, she must have heard something that convinced her to look somewhere else, and went the other way. The door was left door ajar.

I was sat with my eyes fixed on the door, waiting for someone to enter and discover my predictable hiding place. It moved and opened slightly, as if someone invisible had squeezed past it into the room and suddenly the air around me became icy cold. Before I even had time to wonder what was going on, I felt someone blow in my ear. It was the same way that it had happened many times previously, but this time it felt different - not at all gentle, and there was a sound with it too; laughter. I heard it as clear as day; a man, whispering a menacing laughter in my right ear. I could feel him right behind me, almost engulfing my small frame as I froze in fear. Every hair on my body stood on end, and my heart raced. I held my breath so as not to move. I didn't know what was happening but I was incredibly scared. Some-how despite the overwhelming fear, I jumped into action. I clumsily scrambled out from under the table, hitting various parts of my body on the substantial and low table frame as I did, and ran towards the open door. The room was still icy cold, and I could feel "him" following me. His energy was so strong that I looked over my shoulder as I fled the room, as if I would actually see a man running after me, but I didn't. I ran back to the safety of downstairs as fast as my little legs would carry me to find my sisters, still trying to work out what had just happened.

Who was it? Was it all in my head? Maybe I'd been under the table too long and my brain had got bored and invented a story? Did this happen to other people too, or was it just me? I didn't know the answers, but I was terrified, and the empty snooker room had just escalated it's ranking from foreboding, to scariest room in the world!

I was just a child. Most people who are not used to a connection with spirit would find that a terrifying experience at the age of thirty, forty, fifty, and here I was experiencing it at an incredibly young

5

age. I had no idea what to do about it either. I didn't tell anyone, not even my Mum, despite our beautifully close relationship. What would I have said anyway - that I saw the door move and then heard a man laughing in my ear nastily and he scared me? People would just think I had a vivid imagination and tell me it was nothing to worry about, or at least that's what I thought they'd say. So, I kept it to myself and tried to forget about it. As it turned out, that would prove to be a pointless task.

Time passed, as it does, and as I grew, spirit continued to make itself known to me more and more. I felt people brush past me as I was moving about the house. I heard noises that came from nothing, and smelt things I couldn't explain. I saw shadows where there shouldn't have been any. I heard my name called hundreds of times, over and over and over again. I felt energies around me, and by now I had worked out for myself that I could see and hear dead people. I didn't know what to make of it all, and I knew that it wasn't something everyone experienced either, so I kept it to myself in the hope that I wouldn't have to *do* anything, and maybe it would just stop one day. Of course, it doesn't work like that, but I was still very young, and it was the only plan I had.

There were areas of the house I didn't like going anymore, and whenever I could, I avoided them. The small staircase was one of those. It totally freaked me out but I didn't know why. Nothing had ever "happened" to me there, I just had a weird and scary feeling every time I used it. Weirdly, the explanation for that would come many years later when I would be an adult, and meet someone who helped me fill in the blanks...I'll get to that in a bit, promise.

The snooker room still held its title as scariest room in the world, and when I did have to go in there, I tried my hardest to make sure I wasn't alone at least. Even when it was full with the men and women who came to enjoy their hobby in the evenings, I could feel the darker energy I had experienced (many times by now) and chose to stay at the other end of the room away from the door and stage area. Somehow it felt safer down there despite the lack of light from the solid stone wall. The energy was different, so I stayed in the shadows whenever it was possible.

One of the most common occurrences for me at this time, was interaction with another child. She followed me around the house, she sometimes spoke, but I saw her often and felt her beside me daily. I didn't know her name, and didn't give her one. I could sometimes see her walking alongside me, and it was always in the same part of the house too. I wasn't afraid of her but honestly, sometimes she annoyed me which was odd because she was happy, and smiley, and not in any way intrusive. I suppose at that time I just wanted to be left alone and be like everyone else. But I couldn't, and I wasn't, and maybe had I had a better understanding of what was happening to me and how to deal with it, I wouldn't have found her annoying at all. All of these things were happening to me before the age of ten, and knowing that you can see and hear people that are no longer here is a really difficult thing to comprehend as a child. Obviously as an adult, or even teenager, you can access information yourself and discover what it is you actually believe you're experiencing, but as a child that's impossible without asking for help, which I didn't do. My decision to keep it to myself, and my inability to talk to anyone about it, meant that for a long time I believed I was incredibly weird, and probably a bit mad.

When I was eleven, we moved house. We left the snooker club, and moved into a detached house just like everyone else's, in the same town. It was a lovely house and although it had a much smaller garden than we were used to, I loved it. For a long time, there were no whisperings, no cold breezes, no callings of my name, nothing. It was quiet, and for a while I began to think that I'd left all of the dead people behind. Silly me.

Over the next couple of years, I developed a new skill and one that I didn't like at all. I started having vivid dreams and was astonished by how different they felt to my usual ones. Sometimes I would wake up crying and feeling completely panicked about the things that I'd been shown during my sleep, and others I would wake in a calmer state, but with a weird sort of knowing that things weren't quite as they seemed.

I lost count of the amount of times that I had a dream about a certain place, person and event during the night, only to wake up the next day and find myself unexpectedly living out the *exact* re-enactment of it all with *that* person, in *that* place, doing *that* thing.

I remember being about twelve and "dreaming" that my Uncle phoned my Mum in the morning and asked her if we all wanted to go to a certain park for the day. I dreamt about the planning, the picnic, and the big green slide that was there. I dreamt about what my Uncle was wearing, and who went, and how long it took to get there, and every minute detail that you could think of. I remember the colours, the sand, and how it smelt when we were there, and I woke up the next morning knowing that the phone would ring, and it did.

There was a lot of planning. My Mum made the picnic. We went to that park. There was a big green slide. We saw and did all the things I'd dreamt. It smelt exactly as it had the night before, and it was really the first time that I fully understood that this was a very real thing that was happening to me, and not just a whole bunch of coincidences that had just fallen into a convenient line. I was twelve years old, and not only could I see, hear and feel dead people, but now, I also had prophetic dreams.

The darker side of that soon became apparent too. There was a night when I awoke from a terrible dream in which my older cousin had been mugged on the subway. I saw her hurt, and I was really scared. I saw it all happen in my nightmare and woke up very distressed and crying. I had a familiar knowing in the pit of my stomach, and that scared me even more. I went and woke my Mum, and through my tears told her what I'd dreamt. She comforted me, and told me not to worry, and promised she would speak to my Aunty to check on my cousin the next day. True to her word (as always) she called my Aunty who informed her that my cousin had been to hospital after being mugged on the tube the night before. She was ok, but obviously very shaken up. Neither me or my mum knew what to say, so we didn't really say anything. She reassured me that everything was alright and told me not to worry. Looking back on it now, she must have been as freaked out as I was, and probably had all the same questions that I had too.

It wasn't the last time that awful events I saw in my sleep would come to be replicated in life, but it was definitely the time that things started to feel more serious for me. The weight of knowing that I saw terrible events at some point before they happened was terrifying, but I knew there was nothing I could do to stop it from happening.

It had been a while since I'd spoken to, heard, or saw spirit, and with the prophetic dreams happening, I kind of forgot about that side of things. And then something happened that forced me to remember.

9

I'm from a very close family, and a big one too! My Mum has two brothers and a sister, all of who had at least three children each. We all grew up together and my sisters and I, and three of my cousins, spent such a huge amount of time together that we were more like brothers and sisters than cousins. My Nan and Grandad were right at the centre of our family, and we saw them a lot. My Nan was one of thirteen children, and was a very strong, dominant woman. In fact, she was pretty fierce and we didn't mess her around. Despite her sometimes-scary nature, she was really loving and spent most of her time baking and cooking for us all. I loved her to bits. My Grandad was like her antidote. He was fun, and gentle and so mild natured. He always had a smile on his face, and a sarcastic quip ready for you when you walked in. Everyone adored him, including me of course, and he always knew exactly what to say, and when to say it.

My Grandad became ill at some point after we moved house, I don't remember exactly when, or for how long, but it was hard and there came a time when my sisters and I didn't go to see him anymore as it would have been too upsetting. My Mum went to see him all the time; they had a very special relationship, and she told us after one of her visits that he was gravely ill.

Some weeks passed and my Grandad was still with us. It was a day like any other. One of those totally unremarkable days where my Mum had been to work, my sisters and I had been to school and everything just happened as usual. You know the drill; home, tea, bath, bed.

I climbed into bed and went to sleep.

I heard my name, just once. I opened my eyes, and even with my head still on the pillow, I noticed an incredible sense of calm. I sat up, and there at the end of my bed, was my Grandad. He had a cup and saucer in his hands, and he was looking right at me. He had his burgundy knitted tank top on with its big horn buttons down the front, and his tie knotted at the neck of his shirt. He winked at me (it was one of his trademarks), smiled, turned his head and took a sip of his tea, and then he was gone. I knew at that moment that my Grandad had passed away. It was just before three o'clock in the morning. I didn't feel grief, just an enormous sense of peace, so I laid back down and went back to sleep.

In the morning, my Mum came into our bedroom and told us she needed to speak to us. My sisters and I went into the dining room and sat at the table. It was then that my Mum told us that Grandad had died. It was a painful time, especially for my Mum, and of course we were all upset and incredibly sad to have lost him, but for me, there was a peacefulness too. Almost like I knew he wasn't lost completely and was still with us even though we couldn't physically touch or see him.

Our entire family came over that morning, and everyone gathered to share the grief, and to comfort one another. At some point I went upstairs to the toilet, and when I came out, my cousin was coming up the stairs towards me. He asked me if I was alright, and when I said I was fine he added that he was worried about me. I asked him why, and he said:

"Because you haven't cried yet and I'm worried you're holding it all in."

I don't actually remember what I said in return, but I do know it definitely *wasn't* along the lines of:

"No, honestly, I'm fine. I saw Grandad at three o'clock this morning because he came to say goodbye."

That truth was not something I felt able to share so we hugged, and went downstairs together to join the rest of our family. I couldn't help but think about how seeing my Grandad that morning had had such a massive effect on how I was dealing with his passing. It was the beginning of me coming to terms with all the things that I saw, felt and heard, and the event that cemented spirituality into my life, even though I didn't realise it at the time (thank you Grandad).

I kept seeing spirit, kept hearing and feeling things, and more or less kept going as I always had until I was in my mid-twenties. It was at that age when I met a lady who would turn out to become a really significant figure in my life. Her name was Sally, and she opened a shop in the town I had grown up in, moved away from, and had at this time then moved back to. It was my favourite kind of shop... one filled with quirky oddities, old pieces of furniture that had been brought back to life, and lots of vintage loveliness! I loved it, and used to visit whenever I had a chance.

Sally was an interesting woman. She seemed well travelled (it turned out she was), and she had an unusual way about her that intrigued me. She was a healer, and did what she called "Cranial Sacral Healing", something I'd never heard of before, which only heightened my interest.

I got to know her through visiting the shop and spending time there. There was a corner for customers to sit and have coffee. It had a sofa with a big purple throw over it and crazy artwork on the walls. She was friendly, and always made a drink when I went in, so we often sat talking, sometimes for hours and hours at a time.

We talked about all sorts. Spirit, healing, the human condition, and everything in between. It seemed that I had found someone who understood some of the things that happened to me, and it was reassuring and comforting to know that. I still didn't talk about my own spiritual experiences much, I just listened to hers, and it helped.

One day I went to have a look around as I knew from a conversation we'd had earlier in the week that she had been on a massive buying trip. I loved seeing all the new things and where she'd put them. As she started showing me some of the newest treasures in the first room, I heard a strange noise from the bigger one next door. It was like someone had shouted loudly at us, and Sally heard it too. We looked at each other perplexed, and started to walk through to the other room quickly.

When we got in there, there was nothing to see. There was no one there, and no sign of anyone having been there either. There were no cars outside and not a soul to be seen. The lights started wildly flickering, and after more strange noises it became apparent that it was spirit. It was the only time I had experienced spirit making themselves known, and not be on my own. Sally's eyes flickered and I remember her saying something like:

"I'm not having that! They can fuck off if they think they're gonna mess me about!"

It was brilliant and hilarious. This woman was boldly and categorically laying down the law to an unknown spirit that had come in with something that she'd brought on her trip (that was what we surmised). It awoke a realisation inside me that the things I'd had no control over at all, were actually controllable, or at least it seemed, in some way.

As we stood in the room chatting and laughing, I suddenly had an *overwhelming* urge to find something. I didn't know what, but I knew there was something in the room that I needed to seek out. I became filled with emotion and anxiety settled in my stomach. I told Sally and she followed me as I walked slowly around the room. I went to a corner that was brimming with all sorts of different stuff. As we stood next to each other in the cold warehouse-type building filled with curiosities that had once belonged to other people, a strange energy surged through my body and my eyes felt like they might roll back in my head.

"It's in there" I said pointing to a large chest that was underneath a cornucopia of items waiting to be properly sorted.

We started removing things to get to the chest and the closer we got, the more certain I became that something significant was waiting for me inside. Finally, the chest was clear and Sally carefully lifted the lid. There was only one thing filling the vast cavity, and it took my breath away as soon as I saw it. As she lifted the vintage, feather bedspread out of the ancient wooden chest that had carried it here, every hair on my body stood on end and tears welled in my eyes. I still didn't know why, but this beautiful patterned quilt touched my soul in a way I couldn't explain, and Sally saw it happen. She draped the bedspread around my shoulders, and said the most incredible thing:

"I bought this chest and was told that it was empty. I had no idea that this was inside it until now. It's not on any of my receipts, and I've never seen it before. I know that this belonged to a little girl over a hundred years ago. You know her…she used to follow you around when you were little. She says you're her friend, and that you'll remember who she is. Do you?"

I replied, with a certainty that was unexpected to me:

"Yes, I do. Her name is Teresa."

Sally gifted me the bedspread there and then, and I cherished it. Suddenly, something that had been almost unreal, and a secret kept by me for so many years, became...well, real. There was absolutely no way Sally could have known about that ghostly child that followed me everywhere for so long when I was myself only a little girl. I'd almost forgotten it had happened myself! But here I was with an antique bedspread of cream, black, and cherry red, with frayed corners and feathers poking out everywhere, and it all came flooding back. Not only that, but the answer to the question I'd been asking for many, many years also became clear.

Being in possession of the quilt had opened a floodgate of information that flowed to me like a river that had burst its banks. All of a sudden, my brain was filled with images, words, explanations and feelings that I hadn't allowed myself to access before, including a familiar and unwelcome voice...*that* voice. The one that whispered in my ear under the table all those years ago. This time though, it was different. It was like a live action replay instead of the actual voice or energy; enough to tie the strands of a story together, but not enough to scare me in the same way.

Teresa showed me a man, in some kind of all-in-one (like a boiler suit). He was really big. Tall and stocky. He had short brown hair and large hands. I watched the film play out in my mind exactly as she gave me it. I saw my old house, the one where I had been followed and talked to by her for so many years, but I knew that I was seeing something that had happened long before it was my home. The man walked in through the garden, through a door that was no longer in existence when I lived there, with a smile on his face that wasn't a true smile. It was the sort of smile that makes

15

your hair stand on end and fear prickle through your veins. Then she showed me the small cellar under the sister staircase. It was dark, and cold, and looked exactly like it had when I had seen it myself all those years ago. She showed me herself, curled up in a ball, hugging her knees, sobbing silently in the darkness, locked in, and I knew that she had suffered at the hands of this man. A man she should have been able to trust, but one who was not related to her by blood. A man who was there to see her Aunt, who knew of her bad treatment and anguish, but chose not to see. I knew that it was him that ended her life; I saw it in fragments of time and felt it exactly how she had. The fear, the desperation and the intense loneliness and suddenly, it all made sense.

That night in an array of tears, I said sorry to Teresa for not understanding when I was only a girl, and I vowed that I'd never forget her. I released her from this life, and guided her soul towards the light so that she could have the peace she had been asking me for all along. She no longer had to be lonely. She would always be a reminder to me of how sometimes, the things we don't understand only need time and space to become clear, and that real love can overcome any barriers including space and time.

My friendship with Sally became stronger, and even our families spent time together, until such a time that things changed. When I was about twenty-nine, my family and I moved away again. Sally and I stayed in touch at first, but then life took over, and we drifted apart as people so often do.

Sally taught me so much about the metaphysical, and myself, and I will always be grateful to her for creating the space that led me to a new understanding of how things were for me. It's interesting that it was shortly after this time that I shut the doors to spirit for quite some time, dabbling with bits of healing here and there, but generally keeping that door firmly shut, and locked. Until that is, everything fell apart, and I had no choice but to find the key and open it once and for all.

Not Normal Things #1
Seeing & Hearing Dead People
Part 2

It's incredible how much can happen in the space of ten years. It's also incredible just how much of yourself you can hide, or lose sight of in that time too. In the ten years that followed, I had tucked away any parts of myself that were remotely spiritual and chosen to follow a more "normal" path. Ironically, it turned out that my quest to be more normal only threw me into the path of some very Not Normal Things. But after my biggest and most difficult life lesson between the years of 2010 and 2013, things changed in every way, including on a spiritual level. They had to.

In 2012, I started to go to a church group for women. It was a small group that gathered once a week to talk about God, and connect and support one another. Children were allowed too and there was a lovely room full of toys for my then very young daughter to play with, and as there were never more than five or six women there, it was the perfect place to gather my thoughts.

I started going for a reason (a Not Normal reason that I will explain in a different chapter), but without going off track, it's important for you to know that this was a time of significant distress for me.

My life was upside down, and I was slowly losing my mind. I was scared, lonely and desperate, and this group was not just a comfort, but a lifeline. I had isolated myself from pretty much everyone, and was carrying heavier burdens and secrets than I would ever wish for anyone to carry. But it wasn't just the escape from solace and insanity that I loved, it was the conversation about God and Christianity too.

I was brought up as a Christian. I was Confirmed at age eleven, and until I was older, I believed in God, Jesus, Heaven and everything the Bible teaches. But I'd always experienced other things, and I was curious. I wanted to know if they had a place in religion and if so, what that place was. I wanted to know whether the tattoos I was now covered in, really were "bad", and whether the voices and visions of dead people that I'd heard and seen my whole life were accepted in its constitution somewhere. The group was a great place for me to ask those questions, so, I did. The answers were sometimes surprising, and sometimes a little shocking, but always welcome to me and I started to feel more connected to "something" than I had in a very long time. It shouldn't have been unexpected to me that some sort of connection was growing, but taking into consideration the living hell I was in, and my complete disconnection for the ten years previous, it was.

As that connection grew, I found myself unsatisfied with a lot of the answers that I was getting, and was surer still that my path was rooted in something very different. Over the space of a few months, and after a year of attending weekly, I started to go less and less, until, eventually, I stopped going altogether.

The connection that I had buried, or plain ignored, for ten or more years was *desperate* to return to me, and along with the plethora of self-help and wellbeing books that stood on the bookshelves in my new home, there were books about angels, crystals, and anything that was even remotely spiritual. I didn't really know where to start, so I delved in and out of anything that grabbed my attention, and then, one sunny afternoon I was led to the answers that I'd been searching for all my life.

I wish I could tell you what time of year it was, or what the date and time were when I got in my car to visit the junk and antique centre that was about eight miles from my home, but I can't. I don't even know which day of the week it was, but the most important details of that journey will stay with me forever. They changed my life, and I'm not sure whether I can do justice to just how magickal they were as I relay them to you now, but I'll certainly try.

The shop I wanted to visit was a twenty-minute drive. It was in a town on an industrial estate. Not a pretty shop, or indeed a leafy area, but it was great if you wanted to pick up a bargain. So, I locked the front door and climbed into my car. I reversed off the drive, and as I started down the road, the biggest, blackest Raven I'd ever seen flew right in front of my bonnet and let out a deep, loud "caw" as it did so. It was so beautiful, and so close that it made me gasp, and whilst I thought it was a bit out of the ordinary, I carried on with my journey not really giving it much more thought.

I arrived at my destination a short time later and spent a good half an hour or so looking through shelves of household items that other people no longer wanted, and had given away. I measured wardrobes, and cabinets, and rifled through vintage glassware (I've got a mild obsession, and love finding a hidden gem) until I'd exhausted every room. I paid for my new (old) treasures, and went back to my car to start the journey home.

It was busy, and the traffic was heavy. I pulled out of the car park onto the road and stopped at the traffic lights adding my car to the growing queue. As soon as my car was stationary, I heard a loud, singular "caw" and the biggest, blackest Raven I'd ever seen landed *on* my bonnet, *right* in front of me!

I froze, and as I stared wide eyed in disbelief, he turned his head and looked straight at me. Time seemed to stand still. I don't think I even took a breath (for what seemed like an eternity) and then he cawed again, looked away and took off, leaving me bewildered and amazed at what had just taken place.

The lights changed a millisecond later and I was forced to drive whilst trying to work out how the strange encounter had even happened!

A million thoughts went through my head, and I spent the entire journey home muttering to myself in an attempt to cement its fleeting presence into some kind of permanence.

I pulled onto the driveway and carried my now almost irrelevant purchases into the house, still not quite believing what I'd seen.

I decided to make a cup of herbal tea, which I did, and after depositing my favourite mug on to the coffee table in the lounge, I dropped onto the sofa wondering whether I was making stuff up in my head (like I always tended to think I might have when something unexplainable happened).

I sat for a while contemplating the logistics of it being the same Raven. Surely not? There was no way of knowing one way or another, so I gave up.

I wondered what the chances were of seeing a Raven *that* close *twice* within such a short space of time, and what those chances might change to if one of those times *it landed on your car bonnet*!

I had silent conversations with myself about the characteristics of Ravens, Jackdaws, Rooks and every other member of the Crow family to make sure it was actually a Raven, and even though I knew it had been, I Googled it to be sure. I was right…a Raven had flown in front of my car as I left, and within the hour following, another (or the same one – I mean, it's definitely a possibility, right?!) had *landed on my bonnet*!

I got up and stood staring out of the lounge window, amazed and slightly bemused, when out of nowhere, the biggest… blackest… Raven, I'd ever seen… landed right in the middle of my driveway. He looked straight at me, cawed once, and then took flight and left.

My entire body reacted. I had goose-bumps from head to toe. I didn't blink, move or make a sound for at least five minutes. I just stood there, staring at absolutely nothing. I wasn't amazed or bemused anymore; any emotions had been replaced with a certainty that I was on the edge of something incredible. Something mystical and magickal. Something that couldn't be explained or rationalised. Something that was meant only for me. It was as if I suddenly understood that I'd just been gifted the answer to all the questions I'd ever had, and when I realised that, I was spurred into action.

I spent the next few hours immersed in research about Ravens, their mythology, and spiritual meaning, and for the next week I was like a woman possessed! I followed every link, clue, snippet of information, and in the end, despite the myriad of different paths they could have led, there was only one that kept calling my name over and over again…Witchcraft.

In the weeks that followed I drowned myself in anything I could regarding Witchcraft and its origins. I read so much it got a bit confusing at times, but deep within my soul there was a yearning to know more; like I was searching for something that had been lost for hundreds of years. And as time went on, I came to understand that all the things I was reading about were things buried deep inside me, and that living in that way, was more natural to me than breathing. I had found myself, and all the versions of me that my soul had encountered for many lifetimes before, and it was simply breath-taking. I felt free, and for the first time in a long time, very much alive!

In the very early days of my practise I was Wiccan. Many of the laws of Wicca resonated with me, and I suppose it felt more normal to be part of a wider community. It was then that I told my family that I was a Witch, and that I had decided to follow this path. It doesn't sound like a big deal when you say it like that, but for me it felt huge. My Mum, Stepdad and sisters were completely supportive of course, and it felt like a huge weight had been lifted off my shoulders. As it happened, I dropped the whole Wiccan thing after about six months. After stepping more into Witchcraft, and learning more from other people, I knew I needed to forge my own way, and some of the more intricate details of Wicca had uncovered ideologies that I didn't want to identify with. So, forge my own way I did, and I loved (and still do love) every second of it! Finally, I felt I could live my life and go out into the world being one hundred percent myself. I didn't have to dumb down or hide any of the things that I could see, feel, hear or do. That acceptance of myself was like opening floodgates, and as the waves came crashing in, I wholeheartedly allowed myself to be taken by them, and waited eagerly for anywhere they wanted to take me and wow, did they take me!

In the last seven years I have met some *incredible* people and all of them have been part of my learning/remembering process. I've met Witches, Warlocks, Healers, Shamans, Psychics, Artists, High Priestesses, Faerie Queens, some with no such labels, and some with many, and all of who are equally as special. The guidance I received from one of these beautiful souls, gave me more belief in myself than I'd ever had before, and I'm not foolish enough to take that for granted. She showed me how to trust my gifts, and that's not something you can learn from a book. Some of these people are still in my life now, and some are not, but all of them have taught me so much and I am unbelievably grateful.

Today, I do all of the Not Normal Things that I used to try so hard to hide, and I do them every single day of the week.

I read Tarot and deliver messages from spirit. I make potions, moon water and teas. I collect botanicals, feathers, sticks, bones and any odd bits of anything that I think might prove useful one day. I mix odd things together and do spells. I meditate, chant, light code, and talk to the Universe. I dance with my eyes closed and draw sigils in the air. I journal, make vision books and set up intention boxes. I channel when I write, and create with Source. I have visions and prophetic dreams and so much more.

I no longer wait and try to make sense of that which cannot be explained, because I tried that for a very long time, and it just didn't work. So now, *I am* that which cannot be explained. It lives through me and I live through it. There is no longer "a connection" to be found because I am Source, and it is Me; we are one and the same. And it's not because I'm special...I just stopped trying to work it all out and accept it as it comes. I accepted myself. Yes, I was shown the way in, and I did a lot of work after that too, but ultimately it only led me to my own soul, and once you find that, the rest simply happens. The same is true for you too...you *are* the connection! There is no need to try so hard to find something that's already inside you, waiting to be accepted!

Seeing and hearing dead people might not be seen as a very normal thing to be able to do at any age, but I can't imagine being any other way, and it's just one of a long list of Not Normal Things that I'm blessed to be able to experience. I love that little girl who didn't know how the hell dead people could make themselves heard to her, and I am so grateful that she never stopped believing in the impossible. If there's one thing I know from all of it, it's that scientifically, we know nothing of these things at all, how can we? If you accept that we know nothing, you *have* to believe in *anything*, and once you believe *that*, *anything* becomes possible.

P.S.

Do you ever question your own sanity? Have you ever experienced something and convinced yourself that it didn't happen, or that you're a bit crazy and just making things up in your head?

It's happened to me often throughout my life, and whilst I like to think I have it under control, sometimes even now, I have to give myself a talking to and realign myself to my own truth.

Think about all the times that you questioned yourself and the events that made you do so, and imagine if it had been different. Imagine that instead of doubting your own credibility and/or understanding of how things played out, that you stood firmly and trusted your own thoughts, beliefs and feelings. How much surer of yourself would you be by now?! How might things be different in your life? When we solidly show up for ourselves in every situation, good or bad, we experience the kind of growth that shifts everything.

I want that for you. I want you to stop questioning whether what you think, know or feel is true, no matter how unbelievable, and start to trust your inner voice. It doesn't matter what anyone else believes, if it's true for you then, so it is. No arguments necessary, no explaining or justifying, it just "is".

There will always be people who don't believe some of the things I experience and have told you about, but that's ok. I don't need anyone else to believe me. I know what my truth is, and *that* is incredibly powerful. It'll be the same for you too; some people just won't see it how you do, but trust me when I say that it really doesn't matter!

I wish I'd always felt like this. Honestly, it's taken a lot of work to get here; work that I'm so happy I've done, and that I urge you to do too if you need to.

Try it. Take a leap of faith and start today. Trust your own thoughts so that eventually after some practice, you never have to question yourself again. Occasionally, it will get ugly on the journey to your own truth, but I promise it will be the beginning of something beautiful in the end.

P.P.S.

"P.S." = pertaining to its usual meaning "post script" and, for the purposes of this book, "personal study".

Not Normal Things #2
A Paternal Problem

Being Daddy's little girl is something I've never experienced. It's also something that I was always envious of in other people throughout my life. I used to watch girls that I knew growing up, and the way their dads were with them, and think how amazing it must be to feel truly loved by the man who is meant to give you that.

My relationship with my Father is, well… actually, we don't have a relationship now. That was a choice I made after nearly thirty years of trying to overcome the traumas that were part of our history and create some kind of connection, and it wasn't one that I took lightly. I know that there are people who have lost their fathers and who would give anything to be able to pick up the phone and talk to them again, but I've never had that, even when we were in touch. For a long time, I wished it was that way, but eventually I came to the realisation that spending time wishing for something that would never happen was not only deeply saddening, but completely futile and damaging. So, I stopped torturing myself and accepted reality.

I don't have many good memories about my Dad from my childhood. I've tried really hard to think of some, but whenever I think I have, the beginning starts out as something positive and the ending is always tainted with something painful.

I do remember one year though, when I was about eight or nine. It was Christmas Eve and my mum had put my sisters and I to bed. We had put out a plate for Santa and Rudolf with the obligatory mince pie, carrot and glass of milk, and were obviously very excited about Christmas morning. My Mum said goodnight, gave us a kiss (as she did every night), and left the bedroom leaving the door ajar behind her. I fell to sleep until I was woken by a noise at some point late at night.

My eyes blinked open and as I lay there surrounded by darkness, I heard bells jingling. Proper bells; jingle bells! Then, I heard a loud, deep "ho, ho, ho" from above. I froze! I pulled my covers up around my neck and hardly dared to breathe. Santa was *actually* in our house! And I was awake!

Thoughts raced through my head. What if he saw that I wasn't asleep? I wouldn't get any presents! What if I was the one who ruined Christmas for everyone else because I was awake when I wasn't meant to be? What did he *really* look like? Did he *actually* have a red suit? Was I going to get into trouble?

I decided that I had to do my best pretend-sleeping ever, and tried to prepare for the moment that was looming ever closer. The ho, ho, ho-ing got louder and closer until the time came and the door was slowly opening. I was terrified! I don't mean I was a little bit frightened. I mean I was completely and utterly petrified! I couldn't have moved even if I'd wanted to, and try as I might to completely close my eyes, I was way too scared…I needed to be able to see what was happening, and when he had gone.

Through slightly opened eyes I saw him. He was in a red suit with white fur trim just like you see in books and on the television. He had three stockings over his shoulder, presumably one for each of me and my sisters, and as he turned to place one on my bed I saw "it".

Standing incredibly proud from under the fold of his big red hood was an unmistakeable large, and familiar nose. And just like that, the fear subsided and momentary confusion kicked in.

Why was my Dad dressed like Santa? Was he Santa in real life? Was that his job? After a few more minutes, the penny finally dropped, and the story and magic of Santa was lost forever.

I didn't know at the time, but it was the same for my sisters. They were also awake, and they also recognised that infamous nose and lost the myth of Santa that Christmas Eve too. As ways of finding out that Santa isn't real go, it's quite a good one, and my sisters and I have sat together and laughed as we recount the story of the nose and the hood many times. But honestly, it's about the only good or mildly amusing story I can remember of him, and because it stands pretty much alone, that makes even the story itself feel somewhat sad for me.

My perception of my Dad changed when I was about five or six. Something happened that changed the way I saw him for good, and within the same event, my already unbreakable bond with my Mum became even more infallible.

We lived on a busy road. The club (our house) was in the middle of town and on the doorstep of one of the main roads through it. I was going somewhere with my Dad; I can't remember where but that's not surprising as I never made it there anyway. We left the house by the side alleyway and headed to cross the busy road. As we got closer, my Dad asked me to hold his hand and for whatever reason, I didn't want to so didn't. Instead (and genuinely, this is the only bit of this story that I still cannot get my head round) I started to run straight into the road and across it to the other side. I didn't look, I didn't stop or turn around, I just ran. I reached the other side and stood on the pavement waiting for my Dad, quite pleased with myself. He, as you would expect, was not so pleased.

When he joined me on the safety of the pavement, he grabbed my wrist tightly and as my arm swung in the air, he shouted at me telling me how naughty I was and if I ever ignored him again, I'd be in even more trouble than I was already. He swung me round, still holding my wrist too tightly to be comfortable, and almost dragged me back across the road. We walked back down the side alley and through the back door of the house. He was so angry, and I was scared.

He took me straight into the bathroom. It was a big room with a dusky pink carpet. There was a stool next to the bath where my mum used to sit while my sisters and I would play in the extra-large bathtub. My Dad, still grasping my wrist, sat on the stool and turned me round. He pulled whatever clothes I had on below the waist down, and put me over his knee. Before I knew what was happening, he was hitting me over and over with something really hard. I was there for what seemed to me like an age, but in reality, I'm not sure how long it was. What I do know is that I was crying and I was frightened, and he was still striking me with what I had somehow worked out, was my own hairbrush. It was a beautiful hairbrush; a large, thick one with lots and lots of stiff natural bristles. It was made of a dark wood and had my initials in brass letters, nailed to the back of it and I could feel them as they hit my bare skin.

As he struck me, he continued to tell me how I shouldn't have done what I had and how bad my behaviour was, but after a significant amount of time I heard another voice and the bathroom door swung open violently in a whirl of noise and rage. I turned my neck and looked up from the pink carpet where my face had been forced to face, and saw my Mum burst into the room. At the same time as pulling me from my Dad and collecting me into her arms, I heard her say "get your hands off her!" and as she carried me out, I watched my Dad just sitting there on the stool, with my now redundant hairbrush still clenched in his hand.

I don't recall anything else. I don't remember any arguments, or apologies, or conversations about it, it just happened, and then it didn't. I tried not to think about it until many years later, but it was most definitely a significant moment in my life, and in my relationship with my Dad.

After that I felt fearful of him many times. Again, I didn't realise that this was my default position until I was much older and had unwittingly created a very similar environment for my adult self. But I remember many times when I was scared of what his reaction might be to something I did. There was the time I accidentally knocked over and broke a vase he had bought for my Mum and he totally lost it. The time I changed the channel on the TV on a particular Saturday morning and very abruptly wished I hadn't, and so many more. I suppose I learnt to keep my distance really, but I loved him because he was my Dad and I was a child, and there was a much softer side to him too; I just didn't see it that often, and it was hard to remember.

I did see my Dad trying really hard to do good things. I saw him buying my Mum nice gifts and flowers. I knew that he loved her, and her him. I saw him speaking nicely to strangers and people that he knew. I saw those people enjoying conversation with him, and how they clearly thought highly of him. I saw him leave for work every morning and return every night (although not always when expected). I saw my Mum cook meals he liked and how she would try to make him happy. I saw her work really fucking hard, both at work and at home, and I saw her smile, laugh and be kind all of the time. I guess it's the façade that most children believe is their parents' lives, but there was something that always felt different for me too. I felt the undercurrent; I felt the pain he caused and yet, I didn't understand how or why he caused it.

It was on one of those days that you'd never expect to be anything other than familiar, that I came to understand that feeling more, and it was also when everything I thought I knew about my parents, was destroyed.

The town I grew up in had a New Year tradition that we always took part in, as did everyone that lived there. At around eleven pm on New Year's Eve everyone piled into the market square in the middle of town. There was always music playing through loud speakers, and a handful of friendly Policemen who tried to keep their helmets on despite the attempts of alcohol-soaked revellers. It was the highlight of the season, and everyone loved it! Even as hormone filled and usually parentally-embarrassed teenagers, we would walk down with our parents to join in the fun. When it was just before midnight, there would be an official countdown from ten to zero, and then a huge cheer filled the air whilst Auld Lang Syne blasted out over the speakers. Everyone crossed arms, held hands, and sang, even strangers, and it was one of my favourite moments every year. I loved it. It was one of those emotional moments of real, true connection with other people that you rarely get, and I wasn't alone in my fondness of it.

Everything played out just as it always did. We laughed, we got emotional, we sang, we laughed some more and at some point between half twelve and one in the morning, everyone started to filter off home. I was with my Mum and sisters (we had lost Dad somewhere in the melee) and we began walking up through the archway of the local hotel, to our home. It was a ten-minute walk to our front door, and we must have been going for five minutes or so when I turned to my Mum and told her I was going to go and find Dad. I ran back down through the archway lined with cobblestones, and turned around the corner into the market square again. I scoured the remaining crowds of people for my Dad (he was easy to spot because he always wore his kilt on New Year's Eve), and soon found him. He was standing alongside a wall kissing a woman that definitely was not my Mum. I stood and watched for a couple of minutes, my heart racing and my stomach churning as they devoured each other, and as I felt the emotion rise in me, tears fell from my eyes and the air left my lungs. I didn't know what to do. I was fourteen years old and I was watching my Dad do the kind of things with another woman that he should have never been doing. I turned and ran, my heart still pounding and the tears still falling, as I headed for home.

Halfway back I stopped to work out what I was going to do, or if in fact I was going to do anything at all, and then I got really scared. What if my Dad had left now and was about to appear behind me at any moment? What if he'd seen me? What would he say or do? He would definitely be angry and I wouldn't know what to say. I had to get home.

Weirdly, the fear that was now coursing through my veins stopped my tears almost instantly, and I carried on quickly, falling through the front door where I said goodnight to my Mum and went straight up to bed.

I didn't know what to do with the information I had unwillingly gained, and it was a source of great pain and discomfort for me. Every time my Dad gave my Mum a kiss I wanted to cry, and every time she smiled, I felt guilty. I didn't do anything. Instead I tried to convince myself I'd seen it wrong or got mixed up, and as I was used to talking myself into my own insanity (as I've mentioned before), I did a pretty good job at forcing it into obscurity. But as it is with any untruth that is hidden, eventually something happens that forces it into plain sight, and that's exactly what happened. Sadly, for me, it was to take a fairly similar path as it did the first time.

I was fifteen, which means that at least three months had passed, and I got ready for school just like any other ordinary day. I walked to school and when I arrived, I stood in the playground (I always called it that, even at secondary school where little "play" took place) outside my form room. Children who were in the same form as me were milling about, and within a few minutes two girls who were best friends were standing next to me.

I'd like to say that I remember which one of them it was that told me the information that turned my life on its head in that moment, but I can't seem to get a firm hold on it. Sometimes it's one of them, and sometimes it's the other, but the words they said will never be muddled, and if I close my eyes even now, I can still feel my legs turning to jelly beneath me, the sickness that filled my stomach, and the thoughts that raced through my head at a million miles an hour.

There was a village a few miles from the town I lived in. It was a nice village and a lot of children from my form lived there, or close to it. They travelled to school by bus on a busy road that was (and still is I believe) the only way into the town from there without going a very long way round. It was a busy road but in a rural location, and whilst the flow of traffic was always steady, there were many passing places in case you got caught behind a tractor or bus.

I stood talking to the two friends from this village unaware of the significance that the conversation we were about to have would have on my life. They told me about their journey to school, and how a boy in our form was messing about on the bus. It all seemed normal, until all of a sudden it wasn't anymore.

They asked me where my Dad was that morning, and whether he was at work. I told them that he was, and that he had left home at the crack of dawn as he had said he needed to go in earlier than usual. They looked at each other, and said that they'd seen him on the way to school. I said they couldn't have because he worked the other end of town, but they said that it was definitely him, and our car, so I asked them where he had been. They replied that he was in one of the lay-bys, and feeling very confused, I asked them whether they were sure, and what it was he was doing there. One of them (it doesn't matter which one really, but it annoys me that I can't distinguish which, despite all the other detail that I can remember) took a deep breath. They looked at each other, and then she said:

"He wasn't on his own. He was with a boy in our class' mum. They were snogging."

Written down in black and white, it doesn't really sound that traumatic, but as a teenage girl who felt a bit lost anyway, and who had already seen her Dad playing tonsil tennis with a random woman in town by accident three months earlier, it was pretty fucking horrendous.

Like I said before, I remember my legs feeling as though they were about to give way. I remember feeling as though I was going to throw up, and I remember not knowing what the hell to say or do next. It was at that moment that the boy whose mum my Dad was with, turned up.

I didn't know if he knew, and I didn't want to be the one to tell him so, I chose not to. We didn't get on at the best of times, and this was definitely not going to make it any easier. I don't really know how, but I just got on with the day the best I could. I suppose burying the New Year event had made it easy for me to do the same with this new information, so that's exactly what I did. I kept it hidden. I didn't tell anyone, again, and I pretended that everything was just fine even though it most definitely wasn't.

Time passed. Quite a lot of time, or at least it felt that way, and then one day, my Mum sat me and my sisters down and told us that her and Dad were getting divorced. It was heart-breaking. Not so much for me, but for my Mum. Seeing her so hurt and so sad was one of the hardest things I've ever been through, but I knew that she would be ok, better than ok even, and I was relieved for both of us that at some point, I would be able to talk to her about the secrets I had kept.

It turned out that there were many, many skeletons in my Dad's particular closet, and none of them good. There were also too many times to mention in the years after that, that my Dad acted in a way that was extremely emotionally harmful to my mum, my sisters and me. If I told you about them all I'd be here for a very long time, and the purpose of this chapter is not to assassinate my Dad's character, although it's important you understand that his behaviour and choices throughout his life, have deeply affected my reality.

There have been more than several periods in my life when I've tried to rebuild some semblance of a relationship with him, and on one such attempt it seemed to work for a while. He once sent me money when I was desperate without me asking, and one time when I got home from work, he had left a bag of goodies on the doorstep for my children. They were the glimmers of hope that I always clung to, but ultimately, once the clouds roll in again, nothing glimmers like it did when the sun was once shining for that five minutes on a singular day years ago.

Within the walls of my experiences with my Dad, I've felt almost every emotional, and physical response possible. I've felt fear, anger, sadness, guilt and even hatred. I've also felt love, acceptance, forgiveness and understanding, and I'm grateful for all of them.

Late one weeknight about fifteen years ago, I had a one moment of complete love and acceptance that I believe was the start of my healing process around our relationship. It was almost epiphany-like, and although it didn't quite turn out how I expected, I know now that it was the perfect start to what turned out to actually be, the beginning of the end.

I was alone at home (my then husband was working away) and the children were asleep in bed. I had been doing all the things a parent does at the end of a day like picking up toys, washing up the dinner dishes and sorting the washing out. I put some music on while I worked, and got lost in my thoughts. It wasn't long until I found myself thinking about my Dad, and everything that came with that; the hurt, the disappointments, the anger, and the grief that I had felt so many times from the many things that he had done, or not done as the case may be.

I started to wonder why he had behaved the way he had, and how he had chosen to throw away all of the things that he loved the most in his life and that's where I suddenly stopped in my tracks. I thought about my own children, and how much I loved them. I considered what it would take for me to treat them in such a way that would create the same kind of relationship with them, as I had with my Dad. I couldn't comprehend it, and then I started to feel really, really sad. Imagining my own children feeling how I did, was too much, but at the same time it made me think about how *he* might be feeling. Understanding that he might be feeling pain from my actions, no matter why I'd chosen to do them, was almost as painful as some of the things he had done to me. Knowing that I had caused someone else the level of pain that I imagined I would feel if the same was to come about with my own children, was unbearable even though it was purely hypothetical. I was overcome with emotion and after twenty minutes of crying and turning everything over in my mind, I came to the realisation that I had to fully accept my part in our story.

That acceptance meant only one thing as far as I could see, and that was that I needed to apologise to my Dad for anything, and everything, that I had ever done to cause *him* pain. I also knew that I had to make that apology without any expectation of one in return; I was very clear about the fact that this was not about me forcing a "sorry" from him (something that I had wanted from him for a long time) but purely an act of giving, that was sincere and heartfelt to him, from me.

It was very late, about eleven thirty at night, and I wasn't in touch with him at this time although I knew where he lived and had his address. I managed to get his telephone number and standing in my dining room with my bare feet on the wooden floorboards, I dialled the number. My hands were shaking and I had no idea what

I would say, but I didn't falter.

It didn't ring for long and his voice on the end of the line caught me off guard. I said hello and told him who it was. He didn't seem as surprised as I thought he would and I had to remind myself to have no expectations. I took a deep breath and launched into a tearful and genuine monologue about how sorry I was for ever causing him pain or anguish, and that I loved him and even though we weren't in each-other's lives, I wanted him to know that I didn't mean to upset him. I must have said sorry twenty times, and I meant it as much the last time I said it, as I did the first. It was raw, and messy and so fucking real, and when I had finished my emotional ramble, the line was quiet for a second until he said in a calm and clear voice

"I forgive you. It's ok Cate. I forgive you. Ok?"

We ended the call, and I was still stood in the same place in my dining room with my now cold bare feet, still rooted to the same spot. My face was red and blotchy and my nose was running but I was relieved that it was over, and that I had been brave enough to do what I felt I needed to despite all the other messy stuff that *could* have got in the way.

The internal dialogue started.

He forgives me… shouldn't it be the other way around?

No expectations remember.

He didn't say sorry.

No expectations …remember?

He didn't say anything about trying to rebuild things again.

No expectations, remember?!

That night I took responsibility for my part in all of it, and I understood how all of it would have made him feel. It felt better for a while.

Experiencing such a multitude of emotion, pain and healing, can only come from the most difficult relationships we encounter, and despite my previous and eternal feeling of having "missed out" on that whole "Dad" thing, I can honestly say that the one thing Dad did do for me, was gift me the experience of learning and growth.

It wasn't until my latest attempt of reconciliation with him that I finally understood it all and made peace with myself around it. This time it wasn't so gentle though. I had moved from allowing guilt to persuade me into forcing something that was, at its core, genuinely uncomfortable for me, to fully comprehending that in order to heal and move on, sometimes you have to face the ugly and inevitable truth of a situation and allow it to show up exactly as it needs to.

It had been a year or so since I last spoke to my Dad at all, even by text, and I had become more aware of the nagging feeling inside of me that said I should try and make things ok again. I decided to make one final attempt at fixing what was almost beyond repair, so I reached out to him.

The message I sent was very clear. I told him that I hoped he was well, and that no matter what happened, I wanted him to know that I had no ill-feeling towards him and more importantly, that if he wanted to try and sort things out I was willing to do so even though it wouldn't be easy for either of us. The next day, completely unexpectedly (as I hadn't had a reply the day before) my phone rang, and as his caller ID flashed up on my screen, I felt something I hadn't felt for a really long time…rage.

I answered in the kind of tone that says "what the fuck do you want asshole" and as I heard his voice, the fire within me grew. I was *so* angry.

Who the hell does he think he is ignoring that message for twenty-four hours and then just calling me unplanned? (wholly unreasonable of me I know, but that's a really good example of fear showing up as control for you).

He said hello and it felt really awkward. I could tell that he was struggling to know what to say, and I didn't help him. Instead I offered short yeses and nos until it became so unbearably painful to be part of, that I felt sorry for him. I knew that the time had finally come for me to lay it all out on the table and to quote my favourite film of all time, "Let the chips fall where they may".

I told him that I didn't see the point in us trying again even though I felt obliged to, because I knew it would fail. I told him that it hurt me that he didn't know, and seemingly didn't want to know, anything about me. I told him I was no longer willing to paper over the cracks and pretend everything hadn't happened how it had. I told him that the years and years of pain and hurt that he had caused would take a very long time to heal, and even if we tried, I wasn't sure that they ever *could* be healed.

He told me he loved me, and that I was his daughter and that would never change, and in return, I told him that he didn't know what real love was.

He told me that he knew me, and I screamed back at him that he knew nothing about me at all.

I asked him what my favourite colour was. He didn't know.

I asked him what my favourite food was. He didn't know.

I asked him what colour my hair was and again, he didn't have an answer.

Then I was really mean, and asked him when my birthday was. He had seven guesses and still couldn't tell me, so I told him it was embarrassing, and he should just stop.

It was ugly and nasty; I was ugly and nasty. I'd never been that way with him before and it was as much a shock to me, as it was to him.

The years of emotional turmoil surfaced as pure, undiluted rage and I threw it all onto him without a second thought or an inch of remorse, and to be fair to him, he took it all. I wasn't proud of myself, but it was clear that it needed to happen.

Somehow, despite the tension and my incredibly hostile mood, when he asked me if he could try to make it ok, I agreed. We talked about what this would look like and I set firm boundaries. He *promised* me that no matter how difficult it was, (something I had made *very* clear would be the case on lots of occasions due to the nature of some of the discussions we would have to enter into), he would call me every single Friday morning from then on. We said goodbye, and both hung up.

He called the following Friday and we had a weird conversation about nothing much at all, that I wasn't participating in fully. I told him we needed to start at the beginning and he said that was fine, and that he would speak to me the next Friday. He didn't call again for two weeks, and after spending the third Friday watching and waiting for my phone to ring, I decided to end my own pain and I blocked his number. We haven't spoken since.

That was in 2019 when, in my ever-evolving spirituality, I finally understood how to look deeper into other people's responses instead of becoming triggered by them. It's easy to say that we grasp this concept, but the reality is much different, and applying it to the most challenging areas of our lives isn't always easy. Sometimes we like the familiarity of that pain and discomfort. At this time, the ease of accepting my Dad's behaviour came about from two different things. The first of these being the work I did on myself around creating a difference between "reacting" and "responding", and the second was being able to completely remove myself from the situation, and look at *everything* that had happened from my Dad's perspective.

In any of the mentally abusive, or distressing events that happened to me at the hands of my Dad (most of which have been left out of this book), there are signposts. After being thrown around in a whirlpool of confusion surrounding them for most of my life, I suddenly understood *why* he had behaved as he did, and not only that, but I started acting from a place of compassion for myself *and* him.

My Dad has been through significant and life altering trauma in his life. He went through two of the most awful life events you could imagine within the space of a few years, and while he was still a very young man. One of those experiences was something completely devastating that happened to him and my Mum, and the other happened to him whilst they were together. They are not my experiences to share, so I won't, but both of those events would certainly bring about an innate fear of loss for anyone who went through similar. Even though I'd known that he would still be carrying the pain from these events for a long time, it wasn't until I looked at the Not Normal Things that I went through from *his* perspective, that I could see that he was simply reacting to the unhealed trauma within himself, and that was like finding gold dust.

When you have encountered great and engulfing loss like he did, your child running over a main road at the age of five must be the most terrifying experience. As much as my Dad gave me a really bad experience as a result of my actions, that is countered by the fact that I gave him one too. The only difference is that I didn't use what happened to me, and the fear within it, to punish him. Sadly for me, he did, but I know now that the anger he unleashed on me that day came from fear. I also know that fear comes from unhealed trauma, and I can only have compassion for that.

When you are carrying loss around with you every single day, it makes you fearful in every moment, to the point where you don't even recognise it as fear anymore. Sometimes it looks like anger, sometimes it looks like control (as I earmarked above) and sometimes it looks like self-sabotage. Whilst the things my Dad did are awful, and left deep scars that I have had to go through the difficult process of healing, I know now that if he understood *why* he felt the way he did, he wouldn't have done them, and that many of his choices were made from feeling those negative emotions within himself.

Don't get me wrong, I'm not saying it's ok, or that he's made good choices - he hasn't, but I can also see that he is in pain from events that happened years ago, before I was born, and I have compassion for that too.

I do however, also have compassion for myself, and understanding why my Dad acted as he did (does) has given me the power to completely forgive him *and* myself, without feeling forced into having some sort of relationship with him. Ultimately, I have to do what is best for me and my growth. The separation between us always came from me, arguably that's understandable, and even at this point in my life that's the truth, but now it is not accompanied by guilt or shame, and that's incredibly freeing.

I have come to understand that you can have compassion for someone and not have them in your life, and after our last encounter, I was finally able to respond to my Dad instead of react. This might not seem the case given the way it all ended, but if I was to tell you that in the weeks between our last call and the time I blocked his number, I navigated the depths of understanding I've talked about above, and finally released all of the negative emotions I'd been holding onto, you might see it as I do. I didn't send any angry messages telling him why I didn't want anything to do with him anymore, and I didn't cut him out of my life with anything other than peaceful acceptance. I learnt that having empathy for him *didn't* mean I owed him a relationship that effectively, wouldn't be the kind of relationship that I wanted. I also came to truly understand how you can completely forgive someone who has repeatedly caused you great harm and heal yourself whilst doing so. In doing that, I gave us both our freedom.

If I had attempted to write this a couple of years ago, I'm not sure I'd have been able to do it. Reliving everything would have too painful, and back then I really wasn't sure what I thought, or how I felt about it all. There was also a time when I thought I'd never be free from the burden of it; funny how things turn out.

Ultimately, I came to the conclusion that my Dad cannot be the father I *want* him to be, and that it's really not fair of me to keep asking him to try. It's not that I'm better than him, or that he isn't enough for me, but more that our individual understanding of life, and all its lessons, leads us to different ways of being. We show up for ourselves in completely different ways that don't align, and finally, that's genuinely ok with me. He has taught me an incredible amount and gifted me lessons I would never have learnt if things had been different, and for that I am grateful. The only thing I would change if I could, is that he could heal from his own pain and discover the freedom of true happiness, but that is out of my control and I have to trust that his journey through life will be exactly what it needs to be for him...just as not being "Daddy's little girl" has been for me.

P.S.

There are many people who talk about forgiveness, but not so many who talk about forgiving someone *and* walking away from them at the same time. It's popular to tell people that by truly forgiving someone you have to, or should, maintain some kind of relationship with them otherwise you haven't really forgiven them at all. At the risk of being wholly unpopular, and slightly controversial, I want to tell you that that simply isn't true. In fact, in my opinion, continuing a relationship out of duty, and not showing someone the real consequences of their actions, is not only damaging for you but for them too. The tricky part is learning to genuinely forgive *whilst* severing ties (if you feel you need to), and that takes not only courage, but real compassion.

Often, we think that by forgiving someone all we have to do is not give attention to the act that needs forgiving and carry on with our lives. But all that does is bury the pain and breed resentment; a bit like putting a lump of cheese in the back of your fridge and forgetting it's there…it doesn't just sit there and eventually disappear, it grows mouldy and starts to smell until you are forced to acknowledge it again.

True forgiveness lies in releasing the hurt and allowing yourself to honour your true feelings surrounding it. It's perfectly natural to feel sadness, anger or even hatred towards someone who has caused you great pain, after all, we are all having a human experience and all of those things are part of that process. But carrying those feelings around forever only causes more pain for you, and reinforces the impact of the event itself.

You can't truly forgive someone until you've faced your own feelings and asked yourself some difficult questions:

What did they make you feel, and why?

Why does that feeling hurt so much, and where are you still allowing that hurt to affect your life now? Where does it still play out for you? How can you change that?

What do the experiences you had look like from the other persons perspective? (with absolutely no bias for yourself at all!) And what have they had to deal with in their life that has caused them to misunderstand themselves and act in the way they did? What is their suffering, and how must that feel for them?

I have forgiven people in my life of very significant, life altering things and I've done that and walked away from them too. I've crawled away on my hands and knees on occasion if I've had to as well. Sometimes it happens the other way around too; you have to walk away and then you learn to forgive - either way the principle is the same.

I have at times, *wanted* to carry on feeling distain for those people because it was easier than showing them compassion. I get it. Sometimes it's much easier to stay comfortable in your misery than push yourself to do something you initially feel someone else does not deserve. But what I really want you to consider is whether living in that judgement of their actions is beneficial for you? How does it help? The answer of course, is that it doesn't. In fact, it only ever causes more and more pain, whether you realise it or not.

Take a deep breath, think about who you could forgive. The person that you really don't want to think about offering that forgiveness to, should be the very first person you start with. You know, the one you don't want to even give headspace to... start with them.

Imagine how amazing it will feel for you to have a good experience around thoughts of that event or person. Imagine how light and easy you'll feel when you no longer have to avoid anything that might trigger a replay of events. Most of all, imagine how beautiful it would be to want better things and feel true compassion for them.

You don't have to include them in your life. You definitely don't need to be friends with them, or have any kind of relationship with them at all, but you do need to love your relationship with yourself, and forgiving them is a vitally important step in nurturing that.

If you can't see any way of that relationship bringing you joy, or if the damage that they've done is too great a burden to carry, then there is no doubt that you should consider removing yourself from their life. But it's really important to note that you have to do that without resentment for them or judgement of yourself, and with total compassion for both. Otherwise you're just transmuting the pain you released when you forgave them, into something else.

It can feel extra hard to walk away and sever ties with someone that society pressures us into thinking we have a duty to, such as a parent or close family member, but there are ideologies I would ask you to consider that can help challenge that perception and ease your path to feeling freedom around the situation, no matter who it's with.

Have you considered that it's really not fair to expect someone to give you something that they don't have available to them? Every one of us is doing our best, no matter what that looks like, and just because you deem someone's actions as not good enough to fulfil your needs, it doesn't mean that they're not doing their best in that moment. People can only act with the tools that are available to them at the time. That does not mean that every action is excusable, or that people shouldn't be told that they have caused upset or pain; they most definitely should because *that's* the time that they get to choose what to do next. They can choose to grow and acquire a new tool, or stay where they are and experience the same lesson over and over, keeping themselves separate from new, and better, relationships. Either way that choice is theirs, but once you start to see that when people hurt you, it's not because they're "bad" but because they don't have the tools they need to be anything other than what they are in that moment, you can begin the process of choosing what's best for you within that relationship. If walking away happens to be the answer then so be it, but at least by considering how someone is merely on their own journey and maybe hasn't experienced the necessary growth to be where you are in yours, you can walk away with some understanding for them, and why it is the way it is.

I truly believe (and I will no doubt say it many times throughout this book) that love is the answer to everything. There have been many times in my life that holding that belief has challenged me, especially when faced with applying it to those who have hurt me immeasurably, but I have learnt that having love in your heart for everyone *is not* the same as loving everyone as you would those you hold most dear. In the case of people who have caused you trauma, showing love might seem like an incredulous thing to do, but it really isn't that hard. Encouraging someone to grow through experiencing uncomfortable situations is another form of love if it's done with the right intentions. If you love someone, you don't sugar coat things or tell them untruths just so that they aren't upset, and you don't expect them to act in a certain way when they are faced with those situations either. You show them the truth and allow them to step into that, however they need to for themselves. Love has many faces, and in some cases, it simply looks like the space between two people that enables both to move forward with ease and flow.

Walking away from someone, no matter who that person might be, might feel difficult, but long term it's the gift of freedom. It gives the freedom to someone that allows them to show up exactly as they are and not feel the need to change in order to be "good enough". Giving someone permission to just be themselves by walking away is much less damaging than staying and trying to constantly change them.

Giving yourself what you need to thrive is an act of self-love and will improve your sense of worth. It will also automatically set boundaries for the future, so that you don't repeat the same lessons. If removing someone from your life enables you to thrive in this way, and is done without argument, malice or resentment, how can it be wrong?

You can't change what happened, but you *can* change how you view it. Compassion is a much nicer feeling than anger or pain, and the joy of the freedom that true forgiveness brings, can be yours if you choose it for yourself. Equally, walking away from a toxic relationship that you know will never be what you need it to be, is not only incredibly liberating for you, but is freedom for the other person too. You, *and they*, are then able to show up in this lifetime *exactly* as who you are, without having to mould yourself to the expectations and will of someone else, and that is an act of love for both of you.

Not Normal Things #3
A long goodbye
Part 1

I've always been a romantic. I love a great love story, especially one that's a bit different, and I suppose the one thing I always knew I wanted for definite, was to love, and be loved the same way in return.

Weirdly, the boys I liked at school, I was always way too scared to go out with which meant that I didn't have a lot of relationships as a teenager, just a lot of short-lived experiences.

It was that way until I was seventeen, when I was introduced to someone who changed it. We got together, and had been in each other's pockets for a year, and when he asked me to marry him. I said yes, but it wasn't long after that that it all went wrong and I was forced to end things for good. I was devastated and felt like the world had ended but it was, of course, only the beginning.

It took me a long time, but eventually I started thinking about dating again. I got asked out a lot, but I was still scared of getting hurt, so I said no a lot more than I said yes.

I got a job at a newspaper and eventually started seeing a guy that I worked with. It wasn't anything serious, but we had fun and it was definitely what I needed at the time.

One evening we went out and ended up in a popular bar in town. It was packed, and the queue at the bar was at least three people deep, which meant I was standing there for ages when it was my turn to get the drinks in.

I noticed a guy stood the other end of the bar and as I looked at him, he smiled at me. He was really tall and had dark, curly hair and I spent the next ten minutes trying not to let him see that I was trying to catch a glimpse of him. The last time I glanced to that end of the bar, he had gone and I felt noticeably disappointed.

I returned my attention to the task in hand and started rooting around in my purse. A couple of seconds later a man's hand appeared in front of me from behind, and in it, was a fifty pence piece.

"I think you dropped this" the voice said, and as I replied that I definitely hadn't, I turned and saw that it was the guy from the other end of the bar.

As cheesy chat up lines go, it worked pretty well and we spent the next fifteen minutes or so chatting. Soon enough it was my turn to order, and after finally receiving the relevant drinks, I said goodbye and went to find my boyfriend.

A week later and my phone rang at work. I answered and a voice said hello. I had no idea who it was, and after admitting as much to the caller on the end of the line, he replied telling me that we had met in the pub the weekend previously. I was shocked as I hadn't given him my number and didn't quite know what to say, but it felt nice that he liked me enough to track me down. He asked me out for a drink and I explained I was seeing someone so couldn't, but he reassured me it was just for a drink, so I finally agreed, and we arranged it for later that week.

I didn't show up for that drink. I felt bad that I had a boyfriend, and on top of that I didn't know this guy from Adam! He could have been anyone, and I was a little bit scared of that so I decided it was better just not to go. I'd never stood anyone up before, and I didn't like doing it, but it felt way better than the alternative. I didn't have his number to cancel anyway, so I had little choice.

The next day at work, he unexpectedly called once more. I apologised, and he persuaded me to meet up again. It felt nice that someone was paying me so much attention, and had gone to the effort of speaking to me even though he must have felt embarrassed or angry that I had just left him hanging the night before. We arranged another coffee date, and, again, I stood him up.

Again, he called the next day, and again I told him I was sorry but that I'd just had a change of heart at the last minute.

I *really* didn't feel good about the telephone conversations we were having, let alone meeting up with him for a date, and I just couldn't reconcile that within myself. Despite the fact that there was a part of me that loved the attention of this little game we had unwittingly started (that's a really embarrassing thing to admit, and not something I could or would ever entertain now, but back then it was totally true) I knew that if the shoe was on the other foot, and my boyfriend did the same to me, I would be upset. So, I kept saying yes to the mystery man, and then not showing up. We repeated this process a few more times (I know, what a total bitch! Even though I admit that the game had become weirdly enjoyable, it was still totally out of character for me to behave like that even back then!) until he called me and told me it would be the last time. He informed me that if I stood him up again, that would be it. I knew he meant it, I could tell by his voice and I didn't want to risk never speaking to him again, so I agreed to his terms, and the date was set once more.

Things hadn't been going well with my boyfriend (completely unrelated to what had been happening with the mystery man although now I can see that it certainly won't have helped the situation) and I decided that if I was considering going to meet someone else for a drink, I obviously wasn't invested enough to be with him, so I ended things between us that week, just before my date. We weren't serious, and it was no big deal really, but it felt awkward because we worked together, and I genuinely didn't want to hurt his feelings. We managed to get along after that although it was never the same as it had been, which was a shame, but just the way it goes when you're young and don't know the best way to handle it.

Date day came, and this time I turned up. I was really nervous. Going round in circles like we had had built up a kind of pressure that wasn't that fun to be in, but I knew I had to get over it in order to find out one way or another if it was going to go anywhere, so I sorted my emergency get out plan with my best friend, and off I went.

We had a great night, with way too much alcohol, and saw each other again the following day. I was surprised at how well it had gone, and the next few dates went just as smoothly but without the nerves which was a huge relief!

Time moved on, as it does, and soon, we had been seeing each other for a few months.

He lived in a shared house with two other boys, and it soon became clear that they didn't like me being there very much. He found it difficult to strike a balance between seeing me and going out with the lads, but although it made life a bit tricky at times, I was determined not to let that ruin things.

I often felt like he made excuses for the way they were with me, and that caused tension between us. I wanted him to tell them that seeing me was important to him, but he didn't, and instead I got side-lined for a while. I didn't really know what to do about it either. Telling him how I felt only caused a huge row and a bigger divide between us, but keeping quiet was making me unhappy.

After a particularly nasty argument, we met up and talked everything through. He said he didn't want to split up and I told him I didn't want that either, so we found a compromise and gave ourselves three weeks to see if it would work. It did, or it seemed to, but it was obvious he hadn't had the same conversation with his friends, and the tension was still lurking.

One of his housemates took a real dislike to me, and I think he played on that sometimes. When I asked my boyfriend why there was a pair of very skimpy, red, lacy knickers under his bed one day, he told me that they had obviously been planted by the others just to cause a row between us. I wanted to believe him, so I let it go.

I've always felt things very deeply, but the confusion and difficulty I had around that, at the time, was very real and painful, especially given that for the most part, my own experiences of relationships (even as a child) were steeped with the reality of being cheated on. I would spend hours convincing myself that he was telling the truth, that I was making a mountain out of a molehill, and should forget about it. I mean, his friends didn't like me being around *at all*, and that would be a really good way of getting rid of me for good. If they could make me believe that he was cheating on me, then it would be game over, with them as the winners so to speak. But then I'd think back to the nights we didn't spend together, and how he never got in touch at those times. How the next day he would be cagey and distant, and if I said anything, he would blame it on being hungover, and I'd start to believe that maybe he *had* slept with someone else and she'd left her knickers under his bed by accident. I didn't know what know think, so on it went. It carried on going round and round in my head, causing me to become so confused that I just couldn't deal with it. I could have asked him about it again, but I wasn't capable of doing that back then, so I settled for compromising my own feelings by deciding to tell myself I believed him. I buried the whole thing deep enough within in me for it to be easily, and totally, ignored.

As time went on, we met each other's families and friends, things seemed more settled, and I was as sure as I could be, that everything would work out fine.

After a couple of years of me following him around the country (he finished his degree at Uni and moved around to find work), we moved in together, got a puppy, and it wasn't long after that that he proposed. Only a year or so after that, we bought a small house together. It was the first time I had felt really secure, and life felt good.

One weekend, my sister came to visit and to see the new house. She worked abroad on cruise ships which meant we rarely saw each other, so we planned a big night out. We went for dinner and headed to the pub for a heavy night of drinking.

It was warm, and we were stood outside under fairy lights wrapped around some sort of pergola. There was music playing loudly, and the noise of people talking and laughing filled the air. After what was probably way too many drinks, we started talking about the time he had returned to Uni a while after we got together (he was having a year out when we met) and whether we had found it difficult. I said that it had been hard at times, but also went quite quickly, and that the most difficult times where when we had had an argument and couldn't sort it out in person. My boyfriend asked when that had happened, and after giving a couple of examples, I mentioned the time he had gone missing for twenty-four hours and subsequently told me that he had been clubbing and was so drunk he couldn't remember what happened. He laughed, and my sister teased him by saying that he must have known what happened really. He laughed some more before saying that he could. She prodded him into telling us, and he admitted that he had gone home with a girl he met and she had stayed the night. I felt like someone had taken all the air out of my lungs, and after composing myself, and with a degree of confusion, I angrily stated "you cheated on me?!" and fuelled by the bravado no doubt provided by alcohol, he replied "yes".

I was totally devastated, but we were in public, and my sister was there witnessing it all too, so when I got upset and was told that it was a long time ago and didn't mean anything so I should forget it, I dropped it, but I couldn't put it out of my mind.

The next morning, I still couldn't believe what I'd found out. I felt lost and confused, and when I tried to talk to him about it, I was told I was making a mountain out of a molehill and to forget about it. He said it didn't matter, but nothing else mattered at all to me. I was an emotional mess.

The thing is, even *if* I accepted that it was a long time ago and it "didn't matter" like I was being told, it didn't change the fact that he had lied to me. Not just a little lie either, a big one. I kept thinking about how easily he had stood in front of me and told me what I'd wanted to hear instead of what actually happened. I kept thinking about other times he could have lied to me too, and a feeling of complete desperation engulfed me each time. I remembered the red knickers under the bed, and I felt physically sick.

Not knowing what to believe was torturous. What of our life together so far, was true, and what wasn't? All of a sudden, I didn't know anymore, and the only person who could tell me was the one who I'd just found out had been lying to me for years. It was like being in a pool of quick sand; just as I'd manage to get my fear and pain under control and clamber out of the dark, sticky pit I'd fallen into, I'd start to think about it all again and the weight of being pulled back under was too hard to stop. I felt like there wasn't enough air in my lungs…like the sandy silt of the swamp I was slowly drowning in, had somehow already filled them, and I didn't know whether to fight, run, or just give up. I spent a lot of time crying in secret and trying to get some sort of hold on it all, and it definitely took its toll.

I suppose the honest depiction of the outcome, is that I was too frightened of the consequences to do anything about what I'd discovered that booze filled night under the fairy lights, so I did exactly what I was told to do, and forgot about it. Well, that's what I told myself I'd done anyway, but of course it never quite works like that does it.

We stayed in that house for a while, and things weren't always easy, but we managed to get through whatever faced us. I didn't harbour resentment and had accepted my choice to bury what had happened even though it didn't sit well inside me. I had been unwell and was told that if I didn't have children soon, I may not be able to conceive at all. It was hard to hear as I'd always wanted children, but I tried to be optimistic about it and I tried to keep it in perspective. His family didn't like me very much, and they made their feelings well known to us both which was really difficult. On top of that, he wasn't sure which direction he wanted to go in work wise, and was often unhappy about the role he was in, but it didn't seem insurmountable, and we carried on planning the future.

In March 1999, against all odds and after a year of trying, I fell pregnant with our first child, and I was understandably, incredibly happy. It was the start of a new phase in our lives, and even though I knew that everything was about to change forever, I wasn't worried about how that would look, and couldn't wait for it to begin. After a year of seeing negative pregnancy tests every month, finally getting the opposite felt like a true blessing, and I felt like a huge cloud had lifted.

Our son was born on December 17th and he was the best Christmas gift I could have ever hoped for. As is the same with many women during pregnancy, I had put on weight, and although I didn't like myself very much physically, I was deliriously happy that I was a mother, and focused on being the very best I could at it.

We soon realised that a very small two-up, two-down cottage was not the best choice for two adults, a new-born baby and a large dog, so we decided to move. He also took the opportunity to move jobs at the same time, and we ended up moving to the same city as my parents. We made a substantial amount of money on the sale of our house, and chose to renovate an old Victorian semi near the city centre. It was exciting and I was eager to start the process of decorating and designing our new home. I've always loved interior design, and it was the perfect opportunity for me to go a bit mad and really put my stamp on somewhere big enough to take some of the ideas I had come up with.

In the midst of decorating the new house and motherhood, I fell pregnant with our second child. It was June 2000, and our son was six months old. We had been engaged for a couple of years, so decided that we should get married as soon as possible.

The one thing that people who know me really well would tell you, is that I *love* weddings! More than that, I am completely obsessed with wedding dresses, and will happily spend an entire day watching anything on the tv that shows brides-to-be choosing their perfect dress, so planning my own wedding should have been the most exciting time of my life, or at least the most exciting event, but it wasn't.

Aside from the fact that I was pregnant with a baby to look after, planning the wedding just felt stressful. My Mum and Stepdad had given us money to get married, and everything was easy enough to sort out, but I just wasn't excited. We had a huge fall out with his parents which didn't help, but it was more than that. I felt so much anxiety about the whole thing, and even though I loved him and wanted a stable and happy family life more than anything, *something* was in the way. I tried really hard to *become* excited about it, but I couldn't, and I couldn't pin down why (or maybe I didn't really want to).

On the day of our wedding everything went as planned, and we had a lovely day. I was happy that we had got married and hoped that it meant the most difficult times were behind us, which only serves to highlight my ridiculous naivety. But even back then, I would never have referred to that day as the happiest day of my life, and really, it should have been.

I loved my husband, and I was pleased to be married to him, but I felt a deep nagging in my soul that meant I didn't feel fully content or happy. It would be easy to look back now and berate myself for having done something so significant despite it feeling wrong, but there are many reasons for me choosing to ignore how I was truly feeling, and as a result, I have forgiven myself for compromising myself so deeply.

We had children together, a growing family, and I didn't want them to grow up estranged from their father.

As a child, I had watched my Mum compromise herself over and over again to please my Dad, and I suppose to some extent, I thought it was normal. That's not my Mum's fault either by the way, it's one of those things that you don't even know is playing out in your life until it's too late.

Any doubts I had about our relationship always led me back to the decision I'd made to ignore the lies he had told me previously, and as a result of accepting that at the time it happened, I felt I couldn't acknowledge these doubts that niggled away at me now.

It was complicated, and I felt complicated too. I started to tell myself that this was just how it would always be for me, and that it was like that *because of me*, not him. And in a way, that much was true; I mean, I could have left at any time if I really wasn't happy. But I didn't, and I threw myself into family life trying to keep a lid on everything that I felt inside.

Life was fraught with the kind of things that most people experience, as well as some that most don't. The relationship between his parents and me had broken down completely, and that made life very difficult at times. We still saw them on occasion, but it was hard for me to accept that they had said some of the awful things about me that they had, and more so that he didn't stand up for me. I tolerated the visits to their house (they rarely came to us) but often found myself hurt by blatant insults any time I was alone in a room with his father, and quiet snide remarks when everyone else was present. I didn't want to upset the apple cart, so yet again, I stayed silent and carried on. Compromise, compromise, compromise.

Our family dynamic was pretty standard. He worked while I stayed at home. Looking back its easy to see that things weren't quite as they should be, but those Not Normal Things were so subtle at that time, I couldn't even really tell you what they were. What I can tell you is that I felt unsupported in lots of ways, especially where the views of his parents were concerned and I found myself hoping that everything would work out ok in the end. Most of all, I longed to feel truly seen, heard and loved.

In March 2001 our beautiful daughter was born, and I fell completely in love with her, just as I had our son. I was pregnant by August the same year with our third, and agreed final, child. I had a difficult pregnancy and spent a lot of time in bed at the beginning due to complications. I remember sitting in bed watching the news live, when the September eleventh terror attack happened, and watched the second plane hit the tower in real time. It was a worrying time for me with my pregnancy at risk, and my mental health wasn't at its best, but we got through it and in April 2002, our son was born and for the third time in as many years, I instantly fell in love with the chunky little bundle we had created.

My husband had changed jobs again and was working away from home some of the week. It was hard bringing up three children on my own for part of the week, but it was just the way it was, so I got on with it and did the best I could. We had also moved house again due to issues with the area we were living in going downhill. We were often woken up by the police helicopter shining its lights in our bedroom window – well, in the windows of the pub next door actually, but there's little difference, and I was picking up discarded needles from the front garden on almost a daily basis.

We lost a significant amount of money by moving from a house that we had lovingly renovated but that was in a really bad location, but we had no choice, and took the hit. We moved back to the town I grew up in, and although it wasn't what I would have chosen ideally, the house was new and the perfect place to bring up a family, so that was that.

There was so much going on, and I had three children under two and a half which, as anyone who has young children will tell you, is a lot to cope with. With my husband now working away for part of the week, and the financial burden we both faced, we seemed further away from each other than ever. On top of that, I was suffering with a severe case of post-natal depression called Blue Psychosis (the intricate and personal details of which, are for later in the book), and life felt almost impossible despite the joy and magick my children brought.

As time went on, and I started to get better, I hoped that our relationship would also start to recover again, but sadly, it felt very much like the opposite.

I felt very alone at this time, and my husband seemed like a different person altogether. I suppose we were both different people, but he felt so far away sometimes that I found it hard it hard to cope with, especially as all I really wanted was for us to love each other and be happy. I remember my sisters and Mum visiting in late September that year, and me telling them that I felt like we would be getting divorced if things didn't improve. It seemed that life had plans for us that would cement things one way or another, and soon after that, we were both sent into complete turmoil.

In the midst of family life, and heading towards Christmas, our youngest son contracted Meningitis and Septicaemia. He was about nine months old when it happened, and whilst the story surrounding how it unfolded is one that needs to be told, it too is for a later chapter as it has far deeper connections than can be explained in the context of this one. However, for contexts sake, you need to know that our son very nearly lost his life, and when you are told by a consultant, in a room full of maybe twelve doctors and nurses with lights flashing and machines beeping, that your baby might only have three or so minutes to live, it has a massive impact on you, and is definitely something that is "not normal" for most people to experience (thankfully).

It was a moment that I have replayed too many times in my head for various different reasons, but right now I'm retelling it for only one; in that moment, when that an all-encompassing fear rose in my stomach and panic filled my entire being, I needed my husband just as I thought that he would need me too. But it turned out that he didn't, and as he turned without speaking and left the room, I was left alone dealing with everything that was being thrown at me, and navigating my own feelings of utter despair, just had to wait.

I stood and watched as the doctor's stuck tubes, and needles, and medicine into my precious boy. I held in the tears and fear I felt, and I did exactly what I was told, when I was told to do it. I did it on my own, without my husband by my side, and I'd never felt so vulnerable, scared, helpless and alone in my entire life.

It would be easy to say that this was the beginning of the end for me, but if I'm honest, I'm not sure if it was. I tried to understand how he felt, and accepted that he needed to do what was right for himself in that dark moment. But it wasn't easy, and I battled with it for a long time. It only added to the feeling that I was unsupported, and that was something that had been sitting there for years by then.

Our son made a miraculous recovery and life once again returned to its status quo (even though this particular status quo wasn't one I was particularly happy to be in, but it was certainly better than the trauma we had just recovered from). I told myself I should be grateful for the life I had, despite its imperfections and sometimes difficult phases. I tried really hard to make everything as good as it could be, and although my husband and I weren't in the kind of union that I had always wanted, I told myself that it was most people's normal, so everything was fine.

Not Normal Things #3
A long goodbye
Part 2

Six months later and we had two dogs, and with a growing family we decided (because life obviously wasn't quite stressful enough) to move house once more. This time we found the most incredible Victorian house in a nearby town, and everything was in place for us to move. I was completely besotted with the house, and couldn't wait to move in. It felt more like a home than anywhere we had been, and I knew I'd love it just as much once we were in and settled. Once again, life seemed to throw us a curve ball, and a week before completion, the people buying our house told us they wouldn't wait for the date that had previously been agreed, and if we didn't move out straight away the sale would be off. We had nowhere to go, and didn't want to lose the sale, so in a cold and very wet "end of summer", my husband came up with the plan of moving into our tent on a campsite near to the new house. The children were due to start the new school in September and we didn't have enough money to make loads of trips to and from anywhere that wasn't close enough, or to move into a rental house for a couple of months. So, he found a site and we packed everything up that we needed, the rest went into storage, and off we went to camp for as long as it took.

It sounds romantic, but let me tell you it most definitely wasn't. We weren't on a camp site either, but instead a field that a farmer rented spaces out in for events. It had a toilet and an outside sink, but that was it. There was no electric, no shower or washing facilities at all, and it was literally in the middle of nowhere. The weather was terrible. It rained almost permanently and at one particularly bleak point, there was even a tornado (believe it or not it's common for the Fens as it's so flat there).

Every evening I would get the children who were aged four, three and two, ready for bed in the cold, using baby wipes to clean their hands and faces, and every morning I would wake up to a thousand tiny pink worms covering the groundsheet after their successful escape from the water logged ground. That was the first job of the day, removing the worms from the relative safety of our blue plastic floor and returning them to what presumably would be a watery grave.

Crisps and bread became breakfast staples and dressing in clothes that felt cold and damp became normal. It was hell, and I hated every single second of it.

My husband would get in the car and go off to work early so that he could shower once he was there, whilst I tried to entertain the children and keep on top of life in a tent. Most days I tried to get into the town we were moving to, and would spend as long as possible wandering round and using every opportunity I could to charge my phone, get warm, escape the weather, feed the children a decent meal and enjoy time away from the tent. I took them swimming a few times a week so that we could shower, and we became regulars at the park, and supermarket toilets.

Honestly, I can't remember how many weeks we did this for, but it felt like a hundred long, cold, miserable years. I cried often through sheer despair, and whilst I tried really hard to make it so, nothing about it ever felt like an exciting adventure.

I started to resent my husband for going off to work and having a nice warm shower in a clean, private changing room instead of sharing a cold, public one as we did at the swimming pool. I'd watch him drive off and feel anger rising inside me, especially if he seemed in a particularly good mood. Sometimes, quite innocently, he'd text me to tell me what he was having for lunch in the nice warm, comfortable canteen too, and whilst I was pleased he was getting an easy, hot meal and was having a good day, I couldn't help but feel insanely jealous and a little bit pissed off about it at the same time. It was so hard to balance those feelings and not allow them to affect the way I showed up in our relationship, but I never unleashed them on him at all which was good, and in a way, really damaging too.

One morning, in the middle of worm chasing and crisp-dishing-out, my phone rang. It was my Mum, who told me that an elderly family member who I was very close to, had been taken very ill and was in hospital. I was the only person who was close enough to visit, so I spoke to her daughter who also asked me to help her put on her necklace that had been taken off by the nurses, and that she couldn't get back on. I got everything organised, and made the short trip to the hospital.

It was a shock to see my Great Aunty so frail. I'd seen her not too long before that, and although she was clearly older, she had still been as full of as much vigour and mischief as ever. Now she looked different, and it scared me a little.

Sitting with her that day was an honour, but also one of the saddest days of my life. As we held hands, she cried and told me she was scared, and as I put her much loved necklace around her neck, she broke down. Her husband had bought it for her many, many years before, and there hadn't been a day since that she hadn't worn it - until now. As it rested once more against her skin, I saw the relief in her face, and she told me the story of the day it was gifted to her. It was a story of true and very deep love, the kind I'd always longed for, and seeing her face light up as she recounted times passed, awoke a realisation in me that I knew I couldn't run from.

I kissed her goodbye, and told her I'd be back soon, but as I sat in my car ready to leave the hospital car park, I knew I'd never see her again and grief hit me. I cried as many tears as I've ever cried that day. For my Great Aunty, for the sadness I knew everyone who loved her would soon feel, for the loss, and also for a love that I thought I knew, but had clearly misunderstood.

Within the next couple of days my Great Aunty was gone. Everyone was devastated, none more so than her daughter, but even in those difficult times, she gave me a glimmer of hope. With her mum's bungalow stood empty, she called and told me we could move in and stay as long as we wanted. We went that day, but it was incredibly hard for me to be there so soon after my Great Aunties passing, and after a couple of nights, I just couldn't bear to stay any longer.

It was as if all the emotions and difficulties of the past few weeks all came at once. I was completely overwhelmed, exhausted and emotionally wrung out. Despite my husband being there, I still felt very much alone and unable to express just how hard I was finding everything. It's not like we didn't talk, but I felt I had to be strong for the children, and I knew there was nothing either of us could do to change the situation until the sale went through, so yet again, I sat on it all and held it all in.

Luckily, a significant amount of time had already passed and it wasn't too much longer until moving day arrived. I have never been so excited to get into a house in my entire life! We started the arduous but incredibly welcome process of unpacking, and settled in to our new life.

The children started school, I made friends (one of which not only became my neighbour, but one of my best friends in the world) and everything settled down once more.

It felt so good to be secure again, and I was so taken with our new home. It was incredibly beautiful with original features that made it interesting and characterful. I began to feel more hopeful that maybe, despite how far apart we still felt, things might get better and we might be able to finally build a life together where we were both happy.

Three years later the children were settled in school and I'd made good friends. We were fairly close to some of my family and had a well-established life, but despite my hopes for some reconnection between us, my husband was working away more and more, and spent a lot of his time on the road or elsewhere.

Most weeks I was alone for the entire week, with him returning at the weekend. I don't want anyone to make assumptions about my appreciation of what he gave to our family. He worked really hard, and without his income we wouldn't have had the home that we did, the home that I really, really loved. I always knew that, and was always was grateful to him for it. But he chose to seek out work that took him away, and whilst there was no doubt that he loved the children and wanted the best for them, his feelings for me also seemed quite clear, and were not rooted in love but more in a duty that he felt unable to escape from. I also don't want anyone to think I was a total pushover, that's not how it was at all. When we fought, we did it well and we both knew exactly which buttons to press to get the biggest response, but I only chose to argue about the small stuff. Maybe I did that because I was so good at arguing with him, I knew that if I did face the really big and more important issues, that everything I'd been keeping in for years would be unleashed with a ferocity that would burn everything to the ground. Or maybe, I just didn't want to face the fact that I'd made a mess of my life and marriage. That's how it all felt back then, and it was extremely frightening.

We did have a crisis talk though, and heated though it was, it shed light on the fact that he wanted a different job and was desperate to move again in order to have the career that he really wanted, and had worked so hard for. I really didn't want to move again, but I knew that if I didn't, I was putting a nail in the coffin as far as our marriage was concerned, and I would be denying him the opportunity to have the job he longed for, so I agreed. In return for the sacrifice I was making, he promised me that he would find a job where he could be at home more, and that it would ensure that he had significantly more time to spend with me and the children. There was no way I could refuse that possibility, and so it was.

We spent every penny we had, and more, on moving into another beautiful house in Staffordshire. He said that would make travelling easier, work more accessible, as well as presenting better job opportunities for him. It seemed he was right, and soon enough he had landed a great job with a bigger salary that offered him the chance to work from home some of the time. It did still involve him working away, but not as much, and him being around more was at least some consolation for the time he wasn't going to be home.

I'd been clinging to a glimmer of hope that all the upheaval of moving, changing the children's schools and settling into a completely new part of the country would be worth it because it would bring me and my husband closer together. We would discover some kind of love for each other, and everything would be alright. Sadly, I couldn't have been more wrong, and things quickly went from bad to worse.

We lived in our new house for two years, and in that two years my husband began working away more and more. At first, he left on a Monday morning and returned on a Friday evening, but soon enough that changed to him leaving on a Sunday evening, and sometimes even returning on a Saturday morning. We saw little of him. I saw little of him, and even on the weeks that he worked from home, he would lock himself away in the study and only come out to grab what he needed and go back in. He always chose to go to bed much later than me, and was always up earlier.

I didn't realise at the time, but it's obvious now that my heart was breaking a little more every day. I felt let down by him, and also cheated. He had promised me that he would be home more, that we would see more of him. I'd only agreed in the first place because he had promised me things would be different, easier too, but they were so much worse. I was unhappy and out of my depth and trying to talk to him was pointless now. I tried several times and it never ended with a resolution. I was completely exhausted by it all.

No matter how much I tried, he became increasingly distant and we argued constantly. He stayed home alone whenever he got the opportunity, and even at bedtime, he rebuffed any attempts at affection from me let alone any kind of intimacy. It had been many months since we had shared that kind of connection, and I felt the separation deeply.

I decided to try extra hard to make an effort and rekindle some kind of connection between us, so I made a conscious attempt to hold my tongue, make dinners I knew he liked, keep the house spotless, and make myself look extra nice on the days he returned home from being away. I still hadn't got my figure back after my pregnancies, and wasn't confident at all, but I always tried to look the best I could, and hoped it was enough.

He'd been away for a week on my final attempt (not that I knew it was my last effort then), and I'd spent a large amount of money on a new dress and nice underwear to try and make him notice me. It was late when he came in, and the children were already asleep in bed. I heard him put down his keys and start walking upstairs. I was still in the bedroom putting the finishing touches to my hair when he walked in. He didn't look at me so I said hi and waited. He said hello, and walked past me to our bathroom. I asked him how his week had been and he said it had been ok. He came back into the bedroom and I told him that I thought it would be nice if we could spend some time together, and that I'd made a nice dinner. He looked at me, told me he was too tired, and then turned his back and walked out of the room closing the door behind him and leaving me alone, again.

That was the moment I knew it was truly over and there was nothing more I could do.

Over the last twelve years, I have relived that moment many times. It is the moment that I have had to heal from the most, and every time I went back to it, it showed me something new that I needed to work on.

I laid myself bare and made myself vulnerable for the person I thought would never hurt me deeply enough to cause a pain so strong that it would elicit such a vast amount of damage, and would take years to recover from. Sat there dolled up to the nines on our bed, I felt completely humiliated and totally worthless. He had not seen me at all, or even wanted to. He didn't hesitate when he brushed me aside like an unwanted possession. Everything came tumbling down inside, and I couldn't contain the overwhelming sadness that filled me. The tears fell abundantly and silently from my eyes, taking my precisely placed eyeliner with them and leaving puddle-water-coloured tracks down my cheeks. I had nowhere left to go within myself; I was all full up with hurt, fear and grief. I felt so crushed and worse still, I knew I had to see him again that night as the burning smell from the dinner I had spent hours making had made its way up the stairs. I got up, washed my face, got changed (pulling my more comfortable clothes tightly around me as if to keep me safe and hidden), and I went downstairs. We didn't speak to each other again that evening and the next day while he was out, I burnt the outfit and underwear I'd bought specially.

My attempts at any kind of reconciliation stopped that day and I started to notice small things I had previously chosen to ignore, and all the things that I'd chosen to forget about previously, came back to haunt me.

Things like the item of lacy underwear I'd found in the glovebox of our car one day. He told me they had fallen out of his sister's bag when she visited, and he'd put them in there out the way.

Things like the Friday and Sunday nights he spent away from home with work, and how much hotel meal bills had always been for two.

Little things like the way he always shut down his laptop when I walked in the room, or put his phone away suddenly.

Nothing made any sense any more, and I felt unloved, stupid, unattractive, unsupported and worse still, completely and utterly unimportant.

In the week that followed, I discovered that he had lied to me about something *really* big. I found out accidentally from a neighbour, who started talking to me as I was getting out of my car outside the house. I had to pretend that I knew all about it, when on the inside, I was in complete turmoil and had no idea what was going on. Someone had been in our home while he had sent me and the children out, and I had known nothing about it. I asked him about it when I went in, and he lied until I informed him about the conversation I had just had with the neighbour and he had no choice but to admit the truth. It was the final straw, and when the kids went into the garden to play, all hell broke loose.

The weight of almost seven years of feeling neglected, and many more of doubts, flowed out of my mouth, spilling my truths into reality and waxing the seal on the death certificate of whatever it was we had. It wasn't marriage that's for sure, it was an existence, a miserable and less-than-mediocre existence for both of us, and with that outpouring came rage, and a kind of freedom that I hadn't felt for so long, that in that moment, it felt like the only thing holding me together.

That night, whilst laying on my side facing the wall in bed, and after thirteen years together, I told him I wanted a divorce. The words I had thought about speaking hundreds of times before, always when I was in bed, were still difficult to say, but I took a deep breath and allowed them out. I had no other choice. He said ok, and just like that it was over. For the hundredth time that year, I cried myself to sleep as he slept facing the other way with his back to me.

It would be easy to say that none of what happened was my doing, but it wouldn't be true. The children's father wasn't (isn't) a bad man, and I am more than happy to accept my part in the car crash that was our relationship.

I could have left at any time, and I chose not to. I wanted it to work, not so much because of the way I felt about him, but because I wanted the children to have something I didn't have in my father, in theirs.

I kept things bottled up because it was easier than causing conflict, and I knew he wouldn't enter into a reasonable discussion about it anyway, and again, that was totally my choice. It would have been healthier to have faced it all, but I was scared, so I didn't.

Having said that, there is also no escaping the fact that failing to tell someone that you no longer find them attractive, or love them, is not the best way to nurture a happy relationship, and neither is lying to them. Had he been brave enough to have that conversation, I'm sure it would have saved a lot of pain and anguish.

It took me a long time to see what happened clearly, and I think one of the hardest things to come to terms with was that when I looked at it all from the very beginning, it was obvious that from our early dates and onwards, I compromised myself.

I ignored the part of me that knew I was compromising myself in favour of seeing something that, from the beginning, wasn't true. I have no doubt that all those times I pushed thoughts about knickers under beds or in glove boxes to one side, I was ignoring the very thing that inevitably brought our marriage to its knees, and again, that was my choice. Scared little girl that I was. I felt embarrassed that I had been so stupid and naïve, and even more so that I had ignored it for so long.

I wanted that kind of love so badly that I was prepared to completely compromise myself, my feelings and everything I believed in, in order to get it. It just doesn't work like that, and fuck me, did I learn that the hard way.

There were so many times that I felt ugly, unseen, unappreciated, unloved, fat, humiliated, unworthy and utterly invisible in the last seven years of our marriage but what's more scary than that, is that when I started to unravel everything that happened, I felt those things right at the very beginning too. Don't get me wrong, we had fun as well. We laughed, drank, partied, had holidays, had babies, and so many good things, but there were times, even at the start, that I felt that I just wasn't good enough.

In terms of how I see and do things now, that sentence doesn't exist in the same way. I know that if I'm not enough for someone, then it's not that there's anything wrong with me, but more that there's something not right within the dynamic, and that needs to be talked about to be resolved. But back then, I didn't think that way, and for a really long time I felt very deeply that I wasn't good enough and as a result of that, I flogged myself by trying to make it right when it never, ever would be.

Ultimately, no matter what we had been through, I wasn't what he wanted, and no amount of dieting, saving, change of style, effort or moulding would have changed that. I know that now. I wish I'd known it then but that's what lessons are for. We end up in toxic relationships when we ignore red flags and don't stand up for ourselves, and at some point, we need to stop allowing someone else to disrespect and neglect us, by not neglecting ourselves.

I wanted someone to love me, and it seems that I was willing to pay a really high price to stay in something that was never going to give me that, on the off chance that one day things might change.

I ignored every whisper of my soul that told me he was keeping truths from me even in the very beginning, and I blindly carried on compromising my own feelings and beliefs in the process.

My first marriage was a steep learning curve that taught me that I should have stayed true to myself no matter what the consequences. Whichever way you go, the shit is eventually going to hit the fan, so you may as well take the route that keeps your integrity intact.

It taught me what love isn't, and that you can try as hard as you want, but if it isn't right, there's no escaping it – not even by pretending that everything is ok. Especially by pretending everything is ok.

In the end, our relationship was like a really long and painful goodbye, but thank fuck we went through it all. I have the most beautiful, intelligent and amazing children in the world, and through them, I really have experienced a real love that never leaves, and also one that I never, ever have to compromise myself for either.

P.S.

It's can be a difficult task to distinguish the line between "not compromising yourself" and "not compromising", but there's a really big difference between the two. One is completely necessary and the other is wholly unhealthy.

In order for other people to respect you, there's no doubt that you have to know who you are enough to set the right tone within your relationships, and that isn't always as easy as it seems either.

There's no doubt that in the time that I was in a relationship with my first husband, I didn't know who I was at all, and that certainly wasn't his fault. It is also clear that from the start, I compromised myself whilst compromising on all sorts of other things too. Combined, it's not surprising that things turned out the way they did (although accepting that level of responsibility hasn't been easy to do), and if you mix that with some of the choices that he made, and actions he took, we never really stood a chance.

You can't make someone choose to do the right thing, act in a way that supports a happy life, or even make them love you, but you *can* make sure that whatever it is you face, you wholeheartedly support, nurture and stay true to yourself.

I don't want anyone to ever feel the way that I felt during the last few years of our marriage. Feeling completely unseen, unloved and unappreciated is a Not Normal Thing. It isn't normal for the person that is meant to love you, to make you feel that way either by their actions, or lack of them, and is definitely not something you should just accept as "the way it is".

If you know that flinch of pain or panic you get when someone says or does something that hurts or confuses you, and you haven't spoken up about it, you've compromised yourself.

If you've noticed red flags within your relationship, and you've pushed them to the back of your mind or ignored them, you've compromised yourself.

If you've let things slide because you're afraid of losing someone, you've compromised yourself.

How long can you allow those things to happen before it all comes crashing down around you? Well, for me, in the case of my first marriage, the answer to that is thirteen years it seems.

You *have* to develop healthy boundaries around how you want and expect to be treated, and you *have* to make sure that you respect yourself *above* wanting things to work out.

Don't flog yourself by trying to please someone when every action they take tells you that they're not invested in the same way, and if you feel that that is the case, then for fucks sake, voice it! You don't have to shout or say it in a mean way, you can say how you feel from a place of love, but ultimately, saying it in *any* way is so much better than not saying anything at all.

Always compromising yourself because you're afraid of losing someone that you know deep down doesn't want to be with you, just means that you lose them slower. And constantly compromising and always doing things in the way they want to, is equally as bad as never compromising on things too. Does that make sense? I hope so but in the art of being as clear as I can;

Compromising yourself (lowering or altering your beliefs, standards, self-worth, personality, happiness) is never good.

Compromising (meeting someone halfway on things like where to live, paint colours, which restaurant to go to or film to watch) is completely necessary *but* must be done in equal measure by both parties.

It's not up to you to always be the one that bends. And you are worthy of every good thing exactly as you are, no matter what that looks and feels like right now, please remember that.

If you find yourself relating to this, and feel unseen, unloved and unappreciated, then taking a bold step towards mending things means that you might have to face realities you have so far ignored, but if you can love yourself enough to want a happier life, then you can definitely move forward no matter how difficult it might be. Opening yourself up, laying your soul bare, and hoping for someone to respond in a positive way, is a beautiful thing to do and shows bravery and a heart full of love, and no matter what the outcome, things can only get better from there - whatever that may look like.

Check in with yourself. Love yourself. Respect yourself, and by doing so, you'll ensure that other people treat you that way too.

Not Normal Things #4
Depressed, and Deep-Rest
Part 1

There have been many different times in my life when I've thought I was a bit crazy, and I don't mean in a fun "ooh let's go gate-crash a wedding and dance on the tables" kind of way. I mean in a very real "sitting in the dark wondering if things will ever get easier, and if it's all worth it" sense. It has happened for as long as I can remember, because even as a young child I wondered if everyone else thought like I did (albeit it in a less serious way than in my adult years).

I remember the first time depression flirted with me. I was nineteen and my fiancé and I had split up. We had only been together just over a year but I was completely devastated and the world felt like a really bad place. I was still young, especially to have been engaged, and I think people labelled my sadness as just a normal expression of teenage heart-break, and whilst there was obviously an element of that in it, it was much more than that for me.

The night we split up, I went home and crawled into bed, pulling the covers over my head, and with the exception of having to go to the toilet or get something to drink, it was almost a week until I was forced (by an unexpected rescue mission visit from my Mum) to move again. I tried, but I just didn't want to do anything, go anywhere, speak to, or see anyone. Everything felt too hard, and whilst at the time it may have seemed like the over exaggerated self-indulgence of a teenage girl, for me, it was the first time I felt the grasp of the dark and gnarly fingers of depression. Unfortunately, it would turn out to be the least severe, and the first time of many others.

If there's one thing I have learnt about myself in the last nine years since my deep dive into "Self" started, it's that, whilst I have always believed that I am complex and difficult for others to understand, I am in fact an exquisitely simple little soul. That particular untruth I believed about myself, didn't come from nowhere. It was formed from a combination of the opinions of others that I chose to take on board, and my own inherent lack of self-awareness. Fortunately, the excavation works I've undertaken to uncover my true self and reveal Her to the world, has meant that I am no longer under the kind of illusions that make it easier for darkness to fully take control. That doesn't mean that I never feel the darkness creeping in because I do, but I know myself well enough now to recognise its familiar face way before it becomes a serious issue, and that enables me to care for myself in all the ways that form part of the medicine that helps me to beat it from my door. That being said, it still takes work (hard work sometimes too), but understanding the way my brain works, and what my soul needs, means that I at least have some of the tools to do that very necessary work.

Before I write any more, I feel the need to clarify something too. Usually, I would leave this until the P.S. after the chapter, but I want you to be clear on my perspective before you read any further so that you get as much out of the pages that follow as possible.

It's incredibly important for me to tell you that anything and everything I am saying in regards to this, is *my truth*; it won't be the same for anyone else because, gladly, we are all unique. I am not anti-medication and have been on anti-depressants twice in my lifetime, and for a total of approximately nine years. I am not anti-*anything* when it comes to improving mental health. Whatever I've thought might help me in the past, I've tried. Some did help, some didn't, but it won't be the same things for me as it is for others. I am as educated in the science behind depression and other mental health conditions as I am the more spiritual and esoteric perspectives, and don't deny either.

Through years of intense and thorough research, faith in my own divinity, and a lot of trial and error, I am fortunate enough to have discovered and worked out a way to minimise the impact of my own downward spirals, but I certainly don't judge anyone who hasn't got to that point for themselves yet. I am one of you and only have total compassion for your situation, along with a depth of understanding that only those who have experienced the feeling of rock-bottom will ever fully comprehend.

It was within my first marriage, and my third pregnancy in as many years, that I started to experience really significant moments in regards to my mental health. I had already birthed two gorgeous babies into the world (a son, who was fifteen months old and a daughter who was four months old), when I fell pregnant with baby number three. We talked about it and decided we wanted to have our children close together, and I was excited about meeting our new and growing little addition as soon as I found out I was pregnant.

At this point I was an old hand at being pregnant, and in the beginning of my pregnancy, I was confident that everything would be absolutely fine. It was hard work looking after two babies whilst carrying a third, but they were the source of such deep joy for me, that it was never a hardship. I felt incredibly fortunate and grateful to have such perfect and beautiful children, and maybe it was this particular train of thought that led me down what would turn out to be a very destructive path.

At some point within the first six months of my pregnancy, I started to worry about my unborn baby. I would lie awake at night hoping that he was ok, and wondering whether third time around, I would be as lucky as I had already been with other two. I knew from being pregnant twice already, that the kind of thoughts I was having were pretty normal, but that the frequency at which they came and the potency they held, were not. Most women carrying a baby worry from time to time about whether everything is alright, or will be, and whether their baby will be strong and healthy, but in my case, it started to take over and soon became something that filled my busy days as well as my quiet nights. Even when I slept, I was having bad dreams about something bad happening to him, or me, or sometimes both of us. I tried really hard to put it to the back of my mind, but I couldn't stop wondering whether I had had enough good fortune where babies were concerned, and whether this time, my luck would run out.

Looking back now, I can see why I felt that way. My marriage wasn't in the best place, and with the exception of my relationship with my own Mum, the love I felt for the children and received back from them, was more than any I'd ever experienced. I think I was scared of that new connection and love being unexpectedly taken away, but there was also a niggle in the back of my head questioning whether I was experiencing some sort of knowing or foretelling of my own future. Knowing the many visions I'd had up to that point in my life, and that they had mostly come to fruition exactly as I had seen or felt them, scared me because my declining mental health meant that I didn't know how to distinguish between irrational fear, and psychic ability or truth. There was also an aspect of lack of self-worth too. Ask any expectant mother and she will tell you that she loved her baby before she met him or her for the first time, and I was no different, but I didn't think I was good enough for everything to be so perfect the third time round, and almost half expected something to go wrong and that terrified me.

My body was pretty tired after going through three pregnancies so close together, and whilst it could have been much worse, it was protesting a little. I was physically exhausted, and my bump was huge! People often asked me if I was having twins, and there were times I wondered the same myself, or whether I was in fact giving birth to a baby elephant, but my midwife assured me that the reason I was so big was because my body remembered what to do easily, after all, my last pregnancy had only been four months earlier. What no-one thought about, including me, was what effect spending almost two and a half years pregnant might have on my mental wellbeing.

I spent the rest of my pregnancy looking after the two little ones and worrying about a baby who, to all intents and purposes, seemed completely fit, well and healthy at every check-up or scan I attended. It made no difference what anyone said to me, I couldn't shake my concern, but in the middle of April, I gave birth to my third child. It was a really long labour, and when he finally decided to make an appearance, he was completely blue. I freaked out and in a total panic, asked the midwife if he was alive. He was quiet, and hadn't made a noise, but she told me he was fine and that I had nothing to worry about. Seconds later he made a small squeak and was placed on my chest. I spoke to him, and was filled with relief and love. I had another son, and he was absolutely perfect.

My new born was as good as gold and so easy to look after. He didn't cry much at all, and despite being the hungriest baby ever, was incredibly content. He had big chocolatey brown eyes, olive coloured skin and even on the day he was born, his dark curls were subtly evident. I fell instantly in love with him, as I had with my other two children when they were born, and couldn't believe how much I'd worried about him being anything other than perfect.

Within the space of two months, he was so content that I moved him into the nursery to sleep. He was incredibly happy, and slept soundly almost every night which was a total blessing and one that I took advantage of. A full night's sleep for a mother with a new born baby is almost unheard of, but I was gifted that by my soft and gentle natured son, so I made the most of it from early on. For two weeks or so afterwards, everything was fine and I felt better mentally than I had in a while, but then things started to change again. I couldn't have seen it coming at the time, but soon enough, everything that I had felt in my pregnancy would come back with a fierce and renewed vigour. Enough so, that in a relatively short space of time, I would come to hardly recognise myself.

I woke up early one morning and lay in bed listening to the peaceful quiet of the house. I should have been revelling in it as it wouldn't stay that way for much longer with three children, but instead, I felt frightened. Awful thoughts started to run through my head and although I tried to rationalise them I couldn't. I became terrified that my baby had died in the night and that when I went in to get him, I would find him there, lifeless. I knew it was irrational and that there was nothing to suggest that it would happen, but I was overtaken by the images in my head and the thoughts surrounding them. The more I tried to push them away, the louder they became until they were so clear that my heart started pounding harder and faster in my chest, and I couldn't breathe properly. The silence in the house continued, and so did the cacophony of voices in my head whispering hideous words and playing out horrific images. I tried shifting position in my bed and holding my breath, but I couldn't make them stop. Then suddenly, my baby, who had obviously awoken from his remarkably long slumber, made a happy little baby noise. All at once every bad thought and feeling ceased, my heart rate slowed and my breath was easy to catch again. I took a much needed and relieved deep breath, got out of bed, and went to his room. By now he was protesting impatiently as hungry babies do, so I picked him up all the while talking, kissing and smiling at him, and walked down stairs to fulfil my feeding duties, and his empty tummy.

Hearing his voice, albeit baby language, was like coming home after being lost for years. I was instantly soothed, and the panic and fear completely left me. I thought about what had happened and I decided that it was probably normal for some people, even though I'd never experienced it myself before. I was just happy that it was over, and was glad that I didn't need to think about it anymore, and as such, I was completely unprepared when the same thing happened at his nap time later that morning.

Having thoughts that are uncontrollable is scary as hell and utterly anxiety provoking. And trying to put them into any sort of perspective at a time when all perspective has left you, is truly impossible. As an educated woman, I knew that logically, a baby being quiet doesn't mean that it has died, but logic didn't make any difference at the time. It wouldn't have mattered who was with me or what they might have said, the fear that my baby may no longer be alive was overwhelming and felt completely real. The scenarios that played out in my head were enough to curdle your blood, and no matter what I tried, I couldn't make them go away. I should probably have felt a bit silly for even thinking them, but I didn't because the fear of them being a possibility was so strong that it was more powerful than any other thought I was having, and as its grip became tighter, my fear grew bigger and deeper.

Every morning I went through the same. My thoughts would be overtaken once again and I would lie in fear that they might be true. Some mornings, I would ask my then-husband to go in and get him for me, under some pretence of having to do something else whilst he did, so that I didn't have to go into the room. Even then I would sit on the edge of the bed nervously waiting for some kind of signal as to what might come. I told no one how I was feeling as I thought they would just think I was crazy, and also in the vain hope that I would return to a more normal, logical and rational way of thinking soon, but it didn't happen like that at all.

As the days and weeks went by those thoughts got worse and went from being present during just his periods of sleep, to also accompanying his waking moments as well. I quickly became paranoid about someone stealing him, or one of the other two when we were out shopping or at the park, and felt on edge every minute of every day. In daily moments at home, I would find myself having to do things in a certain way for fear of my worst nightmare happening if I didn't. My days were filled with constant fear, worry and compulsions, and my nights were filled with nightmares about what might come to fruition in the future. I was consumed by thoughts of losing one of the children to death, abduction, terminal illness or any other way that might eternally separate us. It was fucking exhausting, and on top of caring for three children under two and a half and running a house, I was on the verge of a complete breakdown.

One of the problems with declining mental health and severe depression, is that you cut yourself off from the people that can help you the most, or at least I did. I stopped calling my mum as much because talking to her without completely losing it and falling in a heap, was almost impossible. I didn't talk to my sisters or friends about it because I didn't want people to think I was being stupid, and I wanted to cope by myself. My independent streak was showing up in really unhelpful and unhealthy ways back then. I didn't know what to do, or who to talk to, and my whole life felt bleak which made me feel extremely guilty. I had three amazing, beautiful and healthy children, a lovely house and no really serious life issues at all, and here I was feeling the way I did. I was ashamed that I thought these things and felt how I felt, and desperately wanted to wake up one morning and feel normal.

That didn't happen either though, and by the September after my son was born, I had become much, much worse. Every morning that I woke up, I wished I hadn't. Every time someone spoke to me, I pretended I was fine and smiled a fake smile, and when I was alone again, my shoulders would drop and I would cry uncontrollably until I had no more tears to cry. My house was immaculate and everything was cleaned until it was pristine and put in its proper place. I'm not sure *anyone* would have known it was a house that was home to three babies, which was unnatural in itself. I read books to, and watched films with, the children, and when they had their naps I would fall into the nearest chair and cry again until I fell asleep or they woke up - whichever came first. I felt alone, desperate and pathetic, and could see no way of anything feeling any easier; except one.

Unbeknown to me, my Mum had begun to worry and phoned my husband. I don't know what it was that she had noticed, but in true mum style she had an inkling that something was very wrong. She had tried to arrange to come and visit, but I kept putting her off and didn't stay on the phone long enough for it to be questioned, so when she spoke to him, they arranged for her to come and see me while he was at work so that she could try and find out what was going on.

It was a sunny morning in mid-September, and once again I had woken up into the relentless nightmare that I had hoped to gain some respite from but had been denied. I went about the morning routine of feeding and dressing the children, making the beds, and putting the washing on. Once the children were all settled and playing happily, I found myself at the kitchen sink washing up and as was always my new, Not Normal way of being now, began trawling through the knitting ball of hideousness inside my head. I thought about the children and how beautiful they were. I thought about how lucky I was to have what I did, and how ungrateful I was for not wanting to stay around to enjoy it all. I thought about people who had lost their baby and would give anything to be in my shoes, and what a total fucking bitch I was for feeling as hideous and low as I did when I had exactly what they wanted. I thought about my husband and how, despite us not being what I wanted us to be, he was a good man and was working hard to give us a good life, and how I should be happy with just having that as it was more than a lot of people ever get. I thought about the washing and the dinner and the bedtime routine, and how no one else would know what to do if I wasn't there to do them anymore. And I thought about how much I loved and adored my children, but it wasn't enough. And in that moment, with those thoughts running through my mind, I put the kitchen knife that I had picked up to wash to my wrist, and pressed the steely tip of it against my skin.

The tears were falling down my face and the deep, primal cries that wanted to escape from my chest were compressed into a wide mouthed and silent internal wail as I slid down the wall of my kitchen, and sat against the cupboard door with the point of the knife still poking threateningly against the pale skin of my wrist. I didn't hear the front door open and shut, but seconds later, my mum was stood before me, and as she bent down to meet me on the floor and uttered the words "oh my darling", I put down the knife and wept in her arms for what seemed like an eternity.

I don't know whether I would have actually carried out what I considered in that moment, but I do know that whatever might have been, my Mum saved me from myself that day in more ways than one. We both cried, and talked, and I told her all of the awful things that had been haunting me since I was pregnant. She loved me despite it all, and we made a plan to get some help.

I saw a doctor that day, and was diagnosed with Blue Psychosis (it might be called something else now as it was years ago) which is a severe form of post-natal depression. I was put on to a high dose of anti-depressants and was assigned a Community Psychiatric Nurse, who would come and check on me daily for the next six weeks to make sure I was getting better. It was the CPN that witnessed the orderly and compulsive way I was behaving, especially when performing tasks like hanging my washing out to dry. She must have seen me do it several times before the day that she challenged me about it, and my reaction to her moving one of the socks I had already pegged out was enough to confirm her suspicions. She asked me why I was so adamant that the sock had to go where it did, facing a certain way and with a specific coloured peg attaching it to the line. When I aggressively told her (after several minutes of cajoling) that I had to because my son would die if I didn't, she made a call and after another appointment the following week, I was officially diagnosed with OCD.

The next few weeks were difficult, but I did start to feel better. The thoughts I had been plagued with eased over time, and I finally started to feel more like myself again.

I was fortunate, even in my depression, because the one thing that wasn't affected by it was my bond with my new born son, or his brother and sister. For many women, that relationship can feel impossible when they are in the depths, and I feel very blessed that it wasn't that way for me. In fact, it was probably the exact opposite for me.

Despite not really wanting to go on anti-depressants, there is no doubt that it had a huge impact, and was most certainly the catalyst for my initial recovery. But what it didn't do, was address some of the deeper issues that surrounded my declining mental health at this time, and whilst I was thankful and relieved to be helped out of the dark hole I was then in, it would be another seven years until I started to face the unpleasant realities that facilitated the grip of the depression that had taken me so wholly. It would however, be less time until I was forced to examine the fear that had overtaken my life for the past year, and really look at some of the more spiritual elements of my personality that I had spent years denying so easily.

Three months went by and everything settled back into place. My mental health was back on track, the children were growing and happy, and life was relatively plain sailing. My youngest son was what you would describe as a bouncing baby boy. His eyes had become darker and more chocolatey and his love for food was unparalleled which meant he had gorgeous thick, chubby thighs and a beautiful squishy face that was almost permanently smiling.

He was still as quiet as he been since the moment he landed earth side, and had worked out that his brother and sister made *great* assistants! He would sit on the floor playing, with them doing their own thing around him, and if he decided he wanted something out of his reach, he would simply point at it and make a noise, and one of them would willingly fetch it for him. It was amusing to watch, and I couldn't work out whether he was just extremely lazy or incredibly savvy.

We often went over to my Mum and Stepdad's house on a Saturday or Sunday to say hello and have dinner. They had a lovely cot all decked out and ready for action in the spare room upstairs so that if any of their grandchildren needed a sleep, they could do so in comfort. One particular such day, my youngest son was ready for his regular early afternoon sleep so I carried him upstairs to take advantage of the luxury accommodation provided by his Grandparents. I tucked him up, turned on the baby monitor and gave him a kiss before going back downstairs.

Sometime later, as I was sat talking and laughing in the dining room, I heard a loud, high pitched squeal over the monitor. I instantly knew something was wrong, and ran upstairs. I turned into the room where he was at the same point that he started screaming more violently, and as I picked him up out of the cot asking him what was wrong, I noticed his thigh was bright red. For a second, I thought he might have been stung by a wasp, but as I was holding him, and right before my eyes, his entire leg suddenly turned completely black. At that moment, I knew something was perilously wrong.

The next few minutes happened so quickly that it's hard to convey them in the way that they unfolded. As I almost sprinted downstairs carrying my screaming baby, I shouted my husband and told him to get the car. He, and my parents had obviously not witnessed and weren't aware of what I'd seen upstairs, and were frantically asking what was wrong. I showed them his leg and said we needed to go to hospital *immediately!* My son was still squealing, his leg still black, and although I didn't know what was wrong, I knew it was serious. My husband started asking me questions, and I screamed at him to just get the car, and a minute later we were speeding to the hospital which fortunately, was only a couple of miles away.

When we arrived, I ran out at A and E while my husband parked. I ran to the desk and explained quickly what had happened while my son lay whimpering in my arms. I uncovered the blanket that I had wrapped him in to show them his leg and was instantly taken into a room where a nurse joined me within seconds. She started asking me questions about how it happened, so I told her, and it soon became clear that she was suspicious of my account. I was showing her his leg and explaining how it had turned black right in front of my eyes, when his other leg which happened to be in her hand, suddenly did exactly the same. She looked up at me, pressed a big red button on the wall, and as a siren called, people appeared from every possible entry point.

Over the next few minutes my baby was surrounded by a myriad of doctors and nurses who were all plugging in machines, sticking in tubes and needles, and talking to each other in a way I didn't understand. There were several different kinds of beeps and lights flashing, and people passing each other equipment I hadn't seen before. I was succinctly told to stay out of the way, at the end of the bed, which felt abnormal and painfully wrong. My motherly instincts were screaming at me to get them away from him, and his now hysterical crying made not doing so even harder to bare. But I knew that they needed to do whatever it was that they were, so I stood watching it all unfold in front of me, feeling utterly helpless and waiting for someone to explain what the hell was wrong.

I didn't have too long to wait and as my husband entered the room and stood behind me, from somewhere amongst the melee, a very important looking doctor came and stood next to us at the end of the bed. He placed his hand on my forearm, and very softly said that our baby had suspected Strep B Meningitis and Septicaemia, and that whilst getting him to hospital so quickly had undoubtedly saved his life in the short term, we should prepare for the worst as he was gravely ill, and they were only expecting him to live for the next three minutes or so. It was right then, that the world stopped turning and my worst nightmare and the thing that had sent me into complete turmoil, seemed to be actually happening.

There are no words that can express just how I felt in that moment. Desperate doesn't cover it. Frightened, terrified or petrified just don't even scratch the surface of the fear that engulfed me. There was an element of disbelief. I couldn't believe that it was happening! How? Why? It was as if time slowed down and sped right up at exactly the same time. My husband didn't say anything at all and left the room. I didn't know where he was going, or for how long for, but at the time, I didn't really have time to think about it too much (that turned out to be something that I would come to care deeply about later on). I didn't cry, or in fact do or say anything at all. I just stood there, at the end of the bed where I had been for however long we had been in the room, and waited for the next three minutes.

Those three minutes passed, and sometime later the atmosphere in the room had calmed slightly. At least six of the doctors and nurses that had initially been involved in my son's care had left, and the few that remained were less frantic. A nice nurse with a soft voice told me that we were being moved into isolation, and that my baby was holding on and was a real fighter. A little while after that, she walked with me down the corridor as two other nurses and a doctor wheeled the hospital bed carrying my baby, behind us. As we walked, she asked me if I was ok. I told her I was fine and as she replied, she touched my arm. She told me that it was ok for me to cry and that I didn't have to hold anything in. She recounted how her and one of the other nurses had talked about how strong I had been throughout the last couple of hours, but that they wanted me to understand that it was perfectly normal for me to not be as composed now the initial shock had worn off. She told me that she was would stay with me if I wanted, but I said that it was ok, that I was fine, and would rather be on my own, so she did as I wished.

The room was weird. It was unusually big, and full of machines and equipment. There were windows all the way down both sides and I could see the nurse's station from the one nearest the door. My son was sleeping with wires and tubes sticking out of numerous parts of his body, and I spent the next couple of hours just looking at his beautiful face and wondering how the hell we had ended up where we were. My thoughts then turned to my husband. I still didn't know where he was, or what he was doing, but as I replayed the moment that he left the room without saying anything, I felt alone and completely abandoned. I understood how difficult it was for him because it was equally as awful for me, but I couldn't understand how he had just left me to cope with it all on my own. It wasn't that I expected him to carry my emotions, or be the strong one, I definitely didn't, but he should have been there so that we could get through it together. And for our son too, he needed us, and I felt angry that he had been so selfish in the moment. After examining it for some time, I came to the conclusion that if he had left the room for a few minutes and then returned, I wouldn't have been upset about it at all, but to not hear from him and for him not to return at all was ...well, almost an unforgivable act in my eyes. With the depth of feeling and sadness that I had around it, I wasn't sure if we would be able to recover, but I consoled myself with the fact that we hadn't even had a conversation about it yet, so there was always a chance.

Not long after that, my Mum came to see us, and I was still ok. No tears were shed and I told my Mum not to worry because I was fine. She stayed for a while and then went back home to look after my other two children. It was about half an hour after she left that something started stirring within me.

Standing in the middle of the room while my baby slept, I looked up at the ceiling. My whole body was flooded with the oddest sensation, like some kind of energetic forcefield was rising through it and building in intensity the closer it got to the top of my head. The emotion started to flow through me too, and as the two collided, there was an explosion that I can only liken to something resembling what I imagine is similar to nuclear fusion. With my face still turned towards the sky, and the feelings surging, I cried out loudly and fell to my knees. It sounds dramatic, and I suppose it was, but it was raw and authentic, and as I knelt on the floor allowing waves of desperation flow through me, thoughts of everything I had feared during my pregnancy and beyond, swirled around my head like a ferocious and unrelenting whirlpool.

I thought about all the times I had been so afraid of my son dying, and all the tasks I had meticulously carried out everyday tasks in a certain way, to try and prevent it from happening. I thought about all the mornings I had been too afraid to go into his bedroom in case he had passed away during the night. I considered the theory that I had manifested everything that was now happening by

100

expecting things to go wrong for so long, and carefully trod the stepping stones through all of those things until unexpectedly, and quite suddenly, it all felt clearer.

With the relief that naturally comes from finally making sense of something that has at one time almost ruined or ended your life, and a small amount of anger at the ferocity of the statement that was being made to me by Source, God, the Universe or whatever name you want to give it, I started to speak out-loud. As the tears once more flowed from my tired eyes, I said I was sorry for thinking and feeling the way I had but that I was only human. I recounted all the times that I *had* trusted in a higher power, and how I didn't need to be tested. I spoke of my belief in all that is and the power of the infinite Divine. I promised to trust in that Divine power to always give me what I needed, and to try not to lose sight of it in anything I faced in the future. I angrily vented how having the mental health issues that I had, didn't make me less spiritual, or less *anything* for that matter, and that I was allowed to be both. It felt like being able to breath properly again, and I realised that even though I had recovered from the events that had led up to that day in the kitchen with my Mum, I'd been carrying the weight of it around with me ever since and had needed to remember something that I had forgotten even existed; my spirituality.

It turned out that my son did have Meningitis and Septicaemia, but with intensive care and medication, he was doing well. That first day in hospital was awful. I was tired and worried, and had no idea what to expect. Although I'd been told he was stable, I was also told that because of the Septicaemia, they didn't yet know if he would lose his legs or not. His blood poisoning was so severe that I was asked by the Consultant at the hospital for permission for photographs to be taken, and still to this day they are used in teaching journals for nurses. It also wasn't clear whether he would need permanent measures to keep his heart working properly either (a stent or a shunt, one or the other, I can't remember), and there was a long way to go before we would be going anywhere. The next morning would bring more answers, and as it happened it brought the much needed and welcome relief that I had been desperate for. He had slept well, everything was going better than expected, and he had woken up early to eat. A nurse brought his breakfast which he demolished in minutes and demanded more of. For the rest of the day, he sat upright in the hospital bed-cot with food in his hand. The whole medical team laughed at his relentless appetite and one of the doctors told me that had it not been for his robust stature, he most certainly would have been overcome by such severe infections. He sat there with tubes and pipes sticking out of him everywhere, eating and acting as if nothing was happening. Fortunately, that trend continued, and it wasn't long before he was out of the woods completely.

The days in hospital all merged into one and I don't recall much after that second day. I don't know how long we were in there for, but it was long enough. I know I didn't leave him, and didn't go home at all while he was there. I don't know how or when we left, when it was that my then husband came back, or even what happened once we got home. I tried for ages to try and access those memories, but they're not available, so I can only presume I don't need to remember them. Or maybe it was only after those first forty-eight hours that the shock of it all really hit me, and consequently, they're tucked away in some archived part of my brain that is looking after them for me. I *can* tell you that miraculously, my son made a full recovery, and his legs were saved. It took him three years to fully recover and for many reasons, his healthy appetite definitely helped speed that process up. He does have a couple of conditions now that have been attributed to this horrendous ordeal, but nothing that is anywhere near as serious. Thank Goddess.

The impact of such a traumatic event has lasting implication and writing about this, even after seventeen years have passed, has been difficult. The images that accompany the events I've described are still crystal clear, and going into such great detail has at times, and probably not surprisingly, brought powerful emotions to the surface. For many years I wouldn't allow myself to "go there" emotionally, but in 2015 I decided that it was time to unpack this particular box. I dived into intense healing sessions with an amazing healer called Ruth Diggles, who also became a good friend, and she helped me to recover from and release the blockages that I had accumulated as a result of shutting it all out for so long.

As for the more spiritual aspects of the whole thing, I learnt huge lessons. I started to understand through everything that happened, that for all of us, there is duality of existence. You can be spiritual without being positive all the time, and if you are living in a spiritual way, acknowledging both aspects of yourself is vital for an authentic and happy life. Duality exists within us all, and denying it makes it much more difficult for anyone to understand how they work, or what they might need.

I also finally became aware that living a spiritually connected life (no matter how big or small a part it plays) is imperative for me, not only in terms of my mental health, but also in terms of how I show up on a day to day basis. As with all lessons, sometimes we remember them, and sometimes they get left by the wayside again for a while. But the foundation that was laid by going through what I did, was solid enough to withstand any abandonment that I temporarily bestowed on it in the future. I planned not to do that of course, but sometimes, best laid plans, go to rest.

Not Normal Things #4
Depressed, and Deep-Rest'
Part 2

My intense experience with that period of depression brought my awareness about my own mental health into the foreground and for the first time in my life, I spent time really analysing some of the less severe, but more constant anomalies that occupied my head space. My diagnosis of OCD was an eye opener, and made sense of *so many things* across my lifetime up to that point. I wasn't to know then, but in years to come, I would also be diagnosed with Autism, and that too would turn out to be an incredibly potent turning point in my understanding of my own mental health and the things in life that felt more difficult for me. That is something that I will talk more in depth about later in the book, but there is no doubt that some of my mental health issues are a symptom of having Autism, and understanding that has helped enormously.

OCD is often spoken about by people who I'm sure aren't meaning to cause offence, but who don't actually realise the severity of the impact it has on those who are diagnosed with it. I would hazard a guess that most of you have heard, or maybe even said yourselves, something along the lines of:

"I'm so OCD...I *have* to have all my cupboards in order with all the tins facing the same way."

I get why people say those things, but the thing is, not *only* does that significantly minimise the very negative experiences that those with OCD have, but it's not even what OCD is!

"Liking" things in a certain way could be deemed slightly obsessive or controlling, but it's not OCD. Having to wash your hands all the time, not liking getting dirty, or excessively checking that your oven is turned off, *isn't* OCD. OCD is all of those things *having* to be done because *if they're not, the person doing them wholeheartedly believes that something really bad is going to happen to them, or someone they love.* There is a *really* big difference, and it's one that is not easy to live with or manage. Can you imagine the amount of anxiety produced by genuinely believing that something *really* bad is going to happen if you don't lock your door three times every time you leave your house? It's all consuming and absolutely exhausting, and nothing like just wanting a tidy and ordered environment.

OCD also has other less well-known symptoms that are equally as difficult to understand and get on top of. In fact, I *still* haven't been able to do that with one such trait whilst the other more widely known ones, such as above, are more manageable for me, most of the time.

All my life I have had weird thoughts at normal times. I know I've said that before, but it's true, and one example of this is easy to explain. I can be walking to the shop on a normal day when I feel perfectly happy and everything is going really well in my life, and with no change in my mood and without any reason whatsoever, a thought will pop in my mind like:

"I could walk in front of that car, it would hit me, and I would die."

The scenes that might follow if it happened, play out in my mind in great detail, and none of it upsets me *or* compels me to actually do it, but I think it.

I could be anywhere, on the platform at the train station, walking alongside a river, driving my car, anywhere, and similar thoughts appear from nowhere and play out in my head. I don't want to actually do them as I have already said, but for a long time, I never understood why they happen and more importantly, I either thought *everyone* had them, or that I was completely crazy. It wasn't until I started paying more attention to my mental health, and in the years that followed when my eldest daughter was diagnosed with OCD too, discovered that we both do it, that I understood it as another symptom. She too thought that everyone had those kinds of thoughts, but after we asked a few people, and saw their obvious confusion/disgust/perplexed expressions when we explained it, we discovered that they didn't. The best thing about this was that all the years of wondering why I had those weird thoughts that seemed completely wrong and incredibly strange, didn't matter anymore, because I suddenly knew that I wasn't alone. In the process of voicing it out loud, it became a less Not Normal Thing for both of us. Sometimes we laugh about them now when we go somewhere together. We might say them out-loud and tell each other what we are thinking and more often than not, the other one will be thinking the exact same thing.

The problem with any mental health issue is that they all feel difficult to talk about. It's especially easy to be embarrassed about admitting that you've wanted to end your own life because there are so many people that don't understand how anyone could ever feel that way. It's often seen as selfish and whilst, again, I can understand how it could feel and appear that way, I can honestly say that anyone who does take their own life isn't being selfish at all. They *truly* believe that their loved ones are better off without them, and that they are doing everyone a service by not being a burden or disappointment anymore. If you feel such a deep lack of love for yourself that you can't accept that anyone else could possibly love you, it doesn't feel selfish but more like a favour. That's probably hard to hear, especially if you've loved someone who has succeeded in taking their own life, and I'm sorry if it is, but it's the truth, (or at least it was for me) and the only way we can overcome the awful stigma surrounding mental health issues is to face the facts and try to understand as much as we can. Covering them up, or pretending they're something else entirely, won't help anyone, least of all those who are suffering from them.

I was on anti-depressants for seven years after the birth of my son, and it wasn't until my marriage broke down and I moved into my own house with the children, that I really started to think about coming off them. I'd tried a few times before but it became clear after a few weeks that my depression was taking hold again, so I was quickly put straight back on them and told to wait a while longer.

Moving out and being out of an environment that was suffocating and made me deeply unhappy, meant that I had started to discover myself, and I was then confident that stopping my medication was the right thing to do. With help from my doctor, that's exactly what I did, and after seven years of relying on them, I finally managed it. It felt incredible, and I was so happy and relieved.

Of course, being able to stop my medication so easily at that time when I had previously been unable to, brought up new realisations that should be noted. For the first time ever, I was not only acutely aware of my own mental health and how important it was, but had also started to really enjoy being me. I was getting to know myself again. What I liked, what I didn't like, and what the things were that made me really happy. I had also removed myself from an environment where I felt unloved, unimportant and utterly invisible, and the synchronicities between that and me finally being free of medication, were hard to ignore. There was no doubt that my initial depression was facilitated by a hormonal imbalance due to pregnancy, but was it possible that I had already been suffering from it when I fell pregnant due to the circumstances and state of my marriage? Were all the times since, that I tried to come off my medication, doomed to failure because I was still desperately unhappy, and felt a deep lack of love? It seemed too likely to be dismissed, and I started to see how vital it is to love and care for yourself.

The leaps I made in that area were evident in the story that I will tell about my second marriage which happened shortly after this period. The difficulties that I experienced through *that* series of events were undoubtedly much worse than those that had occurred during my first marriage, and yet despite not being strong enough to make better decisions for myself during that time, not once did I have to go on medication. Even when I once again had suicidal thoughts, I managed to come through it without chemical assistance, and that demonstrates perfectly just how much difference it makes when you start to understand and love yourself from a place of pure compassion and unadulterated truth. Even the small remnants of love that I had started to bestow on myself in the time between the end of my marriage and meeting my second husband, were enough to see me through those dark times. Properly nurturing your own soul is truly a very powerful thing, and something that I will never again neglect.

In the last eight years I have been on an incredible learning journey in more ways than one. Most of all, I have learnt about what it means to be "Me". I've taken responsibility for *everything* in my life, and the knowledge I've consumed about Spirituality or living a life of connection, I've applied in both theory *and* practice. As a result, I have been able to ascertain certain truths that hold real significance and have great bearing on my own mental health. Through listening to my own mind and body, I have learnt what my triggers are and what it is I need to do to heal those parts of myself, or lessen the effect they have on me. I have come to understand that there is always something to be learnt, no matter how difficult things feel, and that the only way of moving past the dark times is to allow them in and be fully present within them. With that, comes the important realisation that to move forwards, one cannot simply stay still, and from *that* it is clear that there is *always something* that can be actioned to help lessen the pain/toll/sadness/fear. It isn't easy, but then neither is the alternative, so it really is a case of choosing your hardship. I am not the thoughts in my head, just as you are not yours, and discovering the things that help keep you in balance is absolutely key to making any challenging mental health ladder, easier to climb.

As I pointed out early on in the first part of this Not Normal Thing, I don't deny either the scientific facts or spiritual ideologies linked to depression and mental health in general, and it's certainly true that both have aided me in my own journey back to wellness at different points in my life. But I would be denying a part of myself if I didn't pay more attention to the recurring theme that has been at the heart of all of my experiences, whether they were helped by medication or not.

That first mild wrangle with depression that I had aged nineteen was short lived in comparison to the others, but the one thing that I noticed above all else was that I was tired. I don't mean physically. I mean I was tired from a much deeper place, and it was a tiredness that wouldn't abate no matter how long I stayed in bed, or slept. Eventually, that tiredness was overcome by getting up and getting on with life, thanks to a kick up the bum from my Mum at the time, but at no point did I look deeper at why that tiredness happened. As did everyone else, I put it down to the breakup of my relationship, but in reality, it was due to several months of being unhappy *within* that relationship and trying to make it ok when it was never going to be. I had neglected myself and my true feelings to try and save something that wasn't salvageable, or worth saving.

In my next notable date with severe depression, I was savaged by the very real and scientific processes that can happen when your body reacts in a certain way to pregnancy; that is undeniable. But the length that that depression had a hold on me for, and the severity at which I was affected, leads me to believe that I was clinging so tightly to the reins in order to once again save that which was not salvageable, that the hormonal imbalance I then suffered, was enough to send me into a downward trajectory that was more difficult to emerge from as a direct result of being dog-tired to my core. This time I was physically tired in the usual way that most mothers are (I had three children under the age of two and a half), and I was also emotionally tired from ignoring the desires of my soul so obviously, it was a recipe for disaster.

In every other subsequent period of depression, I have been tired. Occasionally I was physically tired as a result of my body's reaction to a condition, but *always* and unequivocally, I have been deeply tired down to the depths of my soul. I take full responsibility for that. It has never been, nor will it ever be in the future, someone else's responsibility to make sure that my soul is nurtured and fulfilled, I see that now. That can only fall to me, and whilst I have wilfully ignored that in the past, it is now always at the centre of everything I do, and every single relationship I have. I am utterly committed to making sure that my souls desires are fulfilled, and that I never suffer from such a deep tiredness of the soul in any part of my future.

Which begs the question; if tiredness was at the core of every experience, was being "depressed" just my souls call for "deep-rest"? And if it was, does the quickest path out of the maze inside our heads become clearer and easier to find when we listen to our souls urges and do *whatever it takes* to nurture it, even if that action seems like the hardest thing in the world to accept?

I am not stupid enough to think that my mental health will be 100% perfect from here on in, and in fact, every day I navigate difficulties due to some of the human conditions I am diagnosed with. Along with that, I am well aware that spiritual growth is always accompanied by challenging periods and awakenings that can feel difficult and painful, but I'm grateful for those. There is no growth to be found in the comfortable. My hope is that by knowing who I am, and what serves me best, I can manage whatever comes my way with as much ease and flow as possible.

For me, there are many things that I can do to ease the noise in my sometimes overcrowded and bewildered brain, but none of those things would have any affect at all unless I was following the path that my soul truly desires and in that sense, I currently find myself in a state of peaceful, and very deep rest.

P.S.

The conversations about mental health are, thankfully, taking place much more frequently and with significantly more intelligence and understanding than ever before. We are seeing high profile people talking about their own personal struggles and how they've overcome them, as well as hearing of the tragic passing of many others. There is much to say on the subject, and even more to learn, which is why I have rounded up some of my own mental health struggles into a Not Normal Thing of their own.

With everyone's needs being different and with everyone suffering through different experiences, the more advice there is available, the more people are likely to be helped. So, with that in mind, I'm going to share some of the practical things and little reminders that help me when I need to gain more clarity, control and insight over my own thoughts. I hope you find something that helps you if you need it, and that long term, you can find a way to coach yourself before things feel too desperate.

Don't do it alone

No matter how stupid or embarrassed you might feel about the way you're feeling, talk to someone. It can be anyone, but *really* try to reach out to someone in your life that you trust and tell them about the stuff that's going on in your head. Somehow, saying it out loud really helps.

Be kind to yourself

You are not the voices or thoughts in your head. You are allowed to feel the way you do, and it's absolutely ok to not be ok. So, cut yourself some slack and talk to yourself kindly whenever you can.

Medication

Quite simply, the most important thing is that there is no shame in going onto medication. It may not be something you *want*, but it could be something that you *need*. If you broke your leg, you wouldn't walk around on it without a cast on because a) it would hurt like fuck and b) it wouldn't heal. Sometimes, it's no different for depression (or any other mental health issue). By all means take advice and make an informed decision, but starting medication is not something to feel ashamed or bad about. There are plenty of people (especially in the spiritual community) who will happily tell you that medication is a bad thing and that if you do the inner work, you won't need it. Whilst this is sometimes the case, it's not always, and more often than not, the people who believe this to be true haven't experienced very severe depression on a personal level. Medication can help you give your soul the deep rest it needs so that you can *then* look at the inner work that you need to. Don't write it off because you think it's not a conscious or spiritual choice to make. In the darkest of times, the best choice for you is whatever helps. If it's any consolation, most modern-day pharmaceuticals have evolved from plant medicine throughout the ages. The medication we take from the doctor now, was discovered through our ancestors use of plants and herbs to do the very same things! Whilst there is obviously a big difference, it's an evolutionary process, and one that

I'm certainly not ashamed of having taken advantage of in the past; and neither should you.

Don't shut the feelings out

Allowing yourself to deeply feel any emotion that comes up is vital in growth and emotional freedom. It's absolutely fine to sit in your pain and sadness for a while, and while you're doing that, take a good look at what's sent you there and try to work out *why* you feel the way you do…that's what emotions are sent for. They're signposts to the lessons and healing we need to work on. The important thing is not to stay there too long. Learn what's needed and then make a plan of action to leave. Thank the emotion on the way out, and once you've done what's necessary to heal, you can shut the door in its face and move on.

Meditate

I know the word meditation makes some people recoil and immediately conjures up an image of a man covered in a sack cloth, sat in the Lotus position with his fingers pinched together and his eyes shut, but it really doesn't have to be that way. Meditation can be a peaceful walk in the park where you try to let go of the thoughts that have been plaguing you. It can be a quiet five minutes while you're standing at the sink washing up and taking a few deep breaths. There are no hard and fast rules, with the exception of making sure that however you choose to meditate (or at least try to), you spend it in as much connection with yourself and your body as possible. Practice is key so try and be consistent, and remember that getting it done is always better than it being perfect.

Nurture your soul

Do the things that make you happy. Whether it's riding a bike, reading a book, going to the shop or *insert relevant activity here. Whatever the things are that light you up and make you feel good, do those. And, if there is something in your life that is dulling your sparkle and making you feel less than you should, look at ways of changing it. Anything is possible if you choose it, and you don't have to do it all at once. *Try to take small steps of aligned action every day* to make it happen.

Take a shower

I know it sounds weird, and I am also acutely aware that when you are gripped by depression, getting in the shower can feel like climbing the tallest mountain, but...try. The cleansing power of water is beautiful, and if you can manage to stand under the comforting cascade of warm water that a shower gives, and really pay attention to how it feels on your skin, it has the potential to clear more than just dirt away. It will make you feel better, and just carrying out that simple act of self-care, is another step in the right direction.

Be mindful of your choices

When you're struggling, the choices you make have significant effects on either improving or worsening your mood. For example, if you feel particularly low one day and decide to play some low tone, slow music, (I find some of Coldplay's stuff particularly depressing) you are much more likely to stay feeling low. If you made a different choice, and put something upbeat and loud on (Bamboleo by The Gypsy Kings for example), you'd find that there would be an improvement in how you feel. Even if you're not dancing on the rooftops, it's much more likely to lighten the load somewhat. The same can be said for the TV programmes you watch or the books you read. Be mindful that you're taking in the kind of material that isn't worsening your mental health or adding to the low vibrational wave you're surfing.

These are just a few things that are available to everyone and that are easy to access. I hope that they help if you should find yourself struggling, and that trying some of them means you can start the process of giving your soul the deep rest it needs.

ꟻNot Normal Things #5
ꟻMeet You by The Ice Cream Vaꞑ?
Part 1

As most Mum's do, mine has always told me stories about her life. She's shared her memories; funny ones, sad ones, interesting ones, and some about our experience together when I was a little girl. We talked often about one in particular. It is the tale of how, as a new mother, she was repeatedly ignored and belittled when she sought advice or help, and how she was worried about me when I was a baby and young child, as she thought there might be something wrong that wasn't obvious. She would relay to me the many times she took me to the doctor asking him to check me over as she believed there was something going on. She recalled how he would look at her as if she was being silly, and then inform her, after having given me a quick check over, that there was nothing wrong with me at all. She would tell me how she took me more times than she could recount over the first few years of my life, and every time the same happened; the doctor would dismiss her, noting that nothing was wrong with me, whilst telling her not to worry and that she was being over anxious. For many years it was just a story that she told me, and one that neither of us had any real explanation or understanding of. Until a day arrived that changed it from being just a tale about a doctor and a mother, and revealed it to be the story of a mother whose instinct was guiding her in exactly the right direction.

I became a mother when I was twenty-five, and by the time I was twenty-eight, I was a mother of three beautiful children. I had my fourth child when I was thirty-eight, and she completed my little gang which then comprised of two boys and two girls. I even did it in sequence (boy, girl, boy, girl), which is something that pleases me greatly and sits well with my somewhat obsessive nature.

Becoming a mother was something I had always dreamt of and it didn't disappoint me. I was (and still am) completely in love with the four humans I had created, and whilst it was far from easy at times, I certainly wouldn't have it any other way. Of course, your first child is always a massive shock to the system in every way! Between the lack of sleep, endless worries about feeding, growth charts, and all the things we have been taught to prioritise in modern society, you also have to realign your relationships, and your entire way of being in the world. No one teaches you that stuff either, and it can feel completely overwhelming at times. But throughout it all, nothing else really matters because you have your baby (or babies in my case), and all of the struggles pale into insignificance in comparison to the love that you feel for them.

My eldest son was a challenging baby in lots of ways. He was unsettled most of the time and cried a lot. He had food allergies and didn't like sleeping much at all. As he grew, it became clear that certain things were more difficult for him to do. He just couldn't learn to ride a bike, and found it difficult to stay still for more than a couple of minutes. On the other hand, somethings came incredibly easy to him and by the time he was one year old, he was not only obviously very intelligent and quick-minded, but fully toilet trained and walking everywhere. Actually, he never walked anywhere; he ran! When he was about eighteen months old, he would trot alongside me on reins for the two miles into town and back without a single complaint of being tired. It was astonishing. He spent hours and hours lining toy cars up from one end of the house to the other, and if they moved even a millimetre, he would have a total meltdown. I would have to leave the perfectly formed line where it was all day until it was time to clear up, and every time I told him it was time to put them away before bed, he would sob furiously. He was fastidious about it, but cars and lines weren't the only things he was obsessive about; from a very early age he had complete fascination with Star Wars, and a bear that he had called Ted (who he couldn't sleep without).

As time passed, other more unusual aspects of his personality became apparent too. He had trouble containing his rage at the simplest things, and also found it hard to concentrate for any length of time. After a discussion with the doctor, we were referred to the mental health team and he went through the usual processes and assessments. A few months later he was diagnosed with Asperger's Syndrome, Sensory Processing Disorder and severe anxiety. He was seven years old at that point, and sadly, the difficulties he faced over the next few years meant that at the age of fifteen, he was suicidal. It was an incredibly difficult time, and I felt completely helpless knowing that there was little I could do to help him out of the hole he was in. Having been there myself some years previously made it harder, and I would have done anything to have taken that desperation from him and harbour it myself instead. I arranged it so that he didn't have to go to school for the foreseeable future, took him to the doctors (which was a total waste of time) and spent hours, days, months, talking with him and offering him any therapies I could find that might work. Two years later he was back on his feet and had also managed to get his GCSE's despite not being in school at all. He worked so hard to get well again, and it was a huge relief to know that he was slowly coming to terms with who he was, and finally learning to love himself.

My eldest daughter was his opposite when she was born. She was very quiet, calm, and unassuming in every way. In fact, she didn't make any real noises at all and by the time she was six months old she had been for ear test after ear test to make sure she wasn't deaf. At her last hearing test when she was about fifteen months old, I was told that she was likely deaf, and that her delayed speech was a result of that. But she had a cold when they did it, so I was instructed to rearrange another test when she was completely recovered. She was referred for speech therapy, and after a solid six months of attending weekly sessions and working with her at home, she started talking. She was still extremely quiet, but it was clear she wasn't completely deaf, and after the therapy, if she wanted to say something, she said it. She didn't ever crawl (she was a bum shuffler) but she also started walking and was fully toilet trained by the time she was a year old. She was completely overtaken with love for a lilac rabbit that she had been gifted at birth. We named him Rabbs and she carried him *everywhere*. She spent her days sat at the bookshelf with Rabbs tucked under her armpit, picking each book off the shelf one at a time, carefully and meticulously reading it, and then putting it on the floor next to her. Once she finished, she would reverse the process filling the bookshelves up again. She was incredibly easy to look after and loved her sleep too. Even as she got older, she rarely cried, and it wasn't until she started nursery at the age of three that her equilibrium was disturbed.

Her first day was an absolute nightmare for both of us. I took her in, put her coat on the hook and we went into the nursery itself where other children were happily playing. I gave her a kiss and told her I would see her later, and as I let go of her hand, she looked at me with her dummy in her little mouth and Rabbs tucked under her arm, and she started crying. She didn't stop crying, and it was heart-breaking as it is for every mum who witnesses the same, but I was told to go and that she would settle down. I returned two hours later to be told that she had not stopped crying, but hadn't made any noise while doing it and had played with the toys on the tables while the tears silently rolled down her face. I picked her up and took her home, hoping that she would find the next day easier. She didn't, and I had the same report the day after that, so I took her home and told her I wouldn't ever take her back there and she could stay with me until she had to start school. She didn't cry again until that day came, and we went through the same process for nearly four weeks until she stopped. It was hellish, and I although I don't regret any other thing in my life, I wish more than anything that I had known then what I know now so that I could not only change *her* reality of that process, but both of her brothers' too.

After years of being largely unaware that her elected silence and attached behaviours were symptoms of a larger issue, it became clear that she was really struggling and after a particularly difficult time in secondary school, I asked her if she would like to be assessed by the mental health team. She said yes, and after a relatively short period of time, she was diagnosed with Autism Spectrum Disorder, OCD and severe anxiety.

Her diagnosis wasn't a shock by the time we got it, and it made it much easier for her to recognise why she was facing some of the challenges she was, and I was relieved that we finally had some answers and could move forwards.

My youngest son was seemingly more neurotypical as a baby. He cried now and then, mostly for food, and slept well. He went to school easily, had no serious compulsions and was good at anything physical. He was also fully toilet trained at a year old, and had no significant motor skill issues or speech problems but had been incredibly ill, and that took some years for him to recover from fully. He had lots of friends at school, was happy to leave me when he went, and had no significant difficulties at all. That all changed when he went to secondary school. Suddenly, he became incredibly shy, anxious and stopped eating. He was relentlessly bullied over a period of two years, and after the attempts of the school and his - by this time enormous (almost six foot nine) elder brother - failed to help, he became so depressed, thin and anxious that we were referred to hospital. Initially, he was diagnosed with Chronic Fatigue Syndrome and we were given information about recovery. School were asked to make adjustments so that he could still attend. They were great, and whilst he kept going, his eating habits became much worse and his anxiety followed suit. He was incredibly low, and after several breakdowns and periods of ill health, he stopped going to school for an entire year and during that time we decided that he too needed to be assessed by the mental health team. Subsequently, he was very quickly diagnosed with Autism Spectrum Disorder, Sensory Processing Disorder, ARFID (Avoidant and Restrictive Food Intake Disorder) and severe anxiety at the age of fifteen. Again, it was a relief knowing that we had something to work with so that he could overcome some of the challenges he was facing, and he felt like he had more of an understanding of himself. He, like his older siblings, said that it made him feel less crazy and would help him accept himself more, and I was grateful for that.

My youngest daughter arrived some eleven years later and by the time she was two days old, it became obvious that she was incredibly attached to me. She was in no way quiet about it either! As long as I was holding her, she was happy, and I had no problem fulfilling that requirement at all. She was given a soft toy when she was a baby and following in her big sister's footsteps, she too formed a significant attachment with it. We named him Ted, and she couldn't, and wouldn't, go *anywhere* without him. By now I was well seasoned in the signs and symptoms that might accompany a child who has Autism, and within the first year of her life, I knew that we would need to start the diagnosis process soon. After another year, and one that was filled with her intense dislike for certain noises, smells, people and places, and her increasingly strong attachment issues, I asked for a referral. We saw the paediatrician when she was exactly twenty-three months old and were told at our initial appointment that a diagnosis of a child under two was almost unheard of, so not to expect one. A week later after the first session of her being observed, the paediatrician told me (on the way out of the room), that although we would have to attend all six sessions there was no doubt that she had Autism, and we *would* be getting a diagnosis despite her young age. Six weeks after that we were given a diagnosis of Autism Spectrum Disorder, Sensory Processing Disorder, severe anxiety, Attachment issues and possible Synaesthesia. It wasn't a surprise at all, but it was difficult to hear. The long list of conditions we were given were significant and life-affecting, and she was just a baby at only two years old. Just as with the other children, it didn't change anything, but it should have meant that we would get some help in overcoming some of the obstacles that were ahead of us. It didn't quite work out that way as it happens, but that's a totally different story, or maybe even another book, and not something I want or need to go into now. I do feel that I need to say something about some of the diagnoses I've mentioned though, in case you don't know what they mean.

Autism is, at a very basic level, a social and communication disorder. It is lifelong, and effects how you interact and cope with the world. These days, most people are aware of Autism and might think that people who have it behave in a certain way and find specific things difficult such as eye contact, rigidity of thinking, liking routine, having an all-encompassing interest in certain things, and in some cases, repetitive movements and gestures. Of course, there are *so* many more defining characteristics and difficulties (which vary in how Autism presents in each individual) but it's important for you to know that not everyone who has Autism, acts in the same way around the same things. What might be difficult for my eldest son, can be easy for my daughter and vice versa. Concepts around food and texture are often challenging, but again, it's not that way for everyone and as I often like to remind people, not all autistic people like Jaffa Cakes.

Sensory Processing Disorder affects how you perceive the senses. For example, bright lights and loud noises can be incredibly frightening, or cause huge amounts of stress, as can certain smells or sights. People with SPD have a more intense perception of these things too and whilst it can be difficult to understand, experiencing the anxiety that can be caused by any of these triggers is overwhelming. Again, it's different for everyone and this is illustrated well in the juxtaposition between how my youngest daughter always feels less anxious when she is surrounded by multiple devices (TV, radio, iPad, and any other sound making machine you can think of) all playing at the same time, whilst my eldest daughter can't cope with that at all and prefers either only one noise, or none at all.

Synaesthesia is less widely known, and up until around forty or fifty years ago, if you were diagnosed with it, it was likely that you were automatically diagnosed with Schizophrenia! No questions asked, no assessments, you were just basically chucked in a straitjacket and thrown in a mental hospital. It makes my heart heavy thinking how many people lived this particular nightmare when what they actually needed was careful nurturing and understanding. The condition itself is the production of a sense impression relating to one sense or part of the body, that is activated by stimulation of another sense or part of the body. I prefer to say that it's like all of the senses talk to each other and get confused. For my youngest daughter this invokes terror which is brought on by unexpected things. To make it slightly clearer I'll give you an example. My daughter can smell colours and hear some of the things she sees (things that don't have any significant noise at all, or any kind of sound that even the keenest ear could recognise). One afternoon my best friend walked into the house wearing a brown t-shirt and completely unexpectedly, my daughter started screaming hysterically! She clamped her hands to her face and shouted "That t-shirt! That t-shirt! Get it away from me! It stinks!!!". She was petrified of it! Luckily my friend experiences her own version of Autism and its co-morbid conditions, and immediately whipped her t-shirt off, stuffed it in her bag and put her bag in the car.

If you think about something simple like a trip to the shops, where you not only experience a more intense level of *all* senses, but they *also* get mixed up and talk to each other, you might have some comprehension of how difficult it is to live with. Or maybe you won't, but either way it doesn't change my daughter's personal experience, and it is only with time, careful management and full-time nurturing that she is learning her own coping mechanisms.

My children are now twenty, nineteen, eighteen and nine. They are the lights of my life, and everything I have ever done, I have done for them; the good and the bad. They are my success story, and my proudest life's work. They are all remarkable in their own way, and I am blessed that their souls chose mine.

My eldest son is the most kind, loving and loyal man who despite his crippling anxiety and reoccurring and often severe depression, works hard to be a light for other people. He's also funny, intelligent, sarcastic and relentless in the pursuit of taking the mickey out of me (something that I partake in happily and give back in equal measure by the way). Anyone who meets him remarks on his impeccable manners and kind nature, and even at six foot eleven tall, I don't think there is a person on earth who would feel intimidated by him (unless he decided they needed to be). He is still finding his way in the world and sometimes becomes overwhelmed with the pressure he puts on himself to find a career path, but I know that he can, and will, achieve absolutely anything he puts his mind to. He is the most perfect example of what well-balanced Divine Masculinity looks like, and I'm sure that will always radiate from him and help illuminate others, no matter what he is doing.

My eldest daughter is still quiet and unassuming, unless she knows you really well, in which case she is happy to display her funny, kind, outspoken and full-of-ideas personality. She is a ridiculously talented artist and although she would argue it to the point of death (she's stubborn too), she is the most creative person I have ever met. She too is funny and sarcastic, and feels everything very deeply. She's a "still waters run deep" kind of person, and I can relate to that more than most. I have absolutely no doubt that one day, when she shows herself to the world, you'll know her name.

My youngest son is still as laid back as he ever was, which seems like a contradiction in terms when he is diagnosed with the things he is, but it's entirely true. He is super cool, funny, goofy (on purpose which is hilarious) and very intelligent. He's a gamer, and he takes great pleasure in telling me that he can react to something that's happening within four hundred milliseconds of it taking place. He too is remarkably kind and caring, and has often helped people less fortunate than him even though doing so has taken him out of his own comfort zone and sometimes caused him great anxiety. He has told me since he was five years old that he is going to build me a house one day, and I have no reason to disbelieve him.

My youngest daughter has grown up with teenage siblings, which means that in more ways than just her neurodiversity, she is not your average nine-year-old. She is sassy, funny, intelligent and fierce. She's destined for the stage and is never happier than when she is entertaining people (on her own terms of course).

All of them have significant difficulties to cope with every single day, and whilst there are incredible similarities between them, they are all enormously different too. No single strategy has worked for more than one of them, and it's been a steep learning curve at times. However, the final appointment I had with my youngest daughter's specialist before her diagnosis (who was one of the UK's leading authority on Autism in girls and women) revealed something that I had long suspected, but not been sure of. It also shed light on why for me, bringing up four children with Autism, had felt so normal, regardless of it being a relatively Not Normal Thing at all.

If you were to ask my Mum what I was like as a child, she would no doubt tell you that I was an angel. I've heard her say it many times as she has recounted stories of my childhood to those that will listen. She would tell you that I was quiet and easy to look after, and would happily play on my own for hours but that if I was away from her, it was a different story altogether. She would tell you how other members of our family or friends would look after me while she had to do something, or go somewhere, and how when she picked me up, they would tell her that I had been crying a lot and had been naughty. She would then quickly advise you that she could never understand the notion that that I was acting in such a way, because I was "such a good girl". She would speak of all the times that I liked to be in the same room as her, and how when I started school, I cried silently every single day for weeks on end. She would voice how my teacher would tell her that I had been really well-behaved, but that my tears had made my books soggy and that I didn't even stop crying whilst eating my lovingly packed sandwiches from my lunchbox. She might also tell you that I had great trouble learning to ride a bike, that I was completely obsessed by horses and never stopped asking for one at every Christmas (I still do that, and for my birthday), and how I had favourite clothes that I would want to wear over and over again. How all I drank was orange squash, and that if I got upset, the only way to stop me crying was to put me to bed (no matter what the time of day, or my age) and let me sleep because it was only when she did that, that the tears would stop. You would hear a thousand stories about the countless times she repeated the words "put something on your feet" or "will you get your shoes on if you're going outside" and how I would do so until I was out of sight, but then adeptly remove them again so I could be barefoot once more.

If you asked her what I was like as a teenager, she'd probably tell you that she was worried about me because I drank too much, and that I had a tendency to copy the people I surrounded myself with. She would tell you that she had to remove my hands from my face a hundred times a day because I would be pressing in the side of my mouth, and it drove her mad. She would probably tell you that I still loved horses, and being barefoot. You might be told that I had a massive (I mean MASSIVE) problem with Maths, and that despite having a private tutor out of school, I simply could not understand numbers. I'm also pretty sure that you'd hear about the volume that I always played my music at, which seemed unusually higher than even the most raucous of teenagers.

If you asked her what I was like as a person, she would tell you that I'm kind and loving, and extremely sensitive. She would fill your ears with tales about lovely things that I'd done, and how I care deeply about people, animals and more or less everything. She'd also tell you that I was different, and whilst she had always felt that way, she didn't really know how, or why.

My youngest daughter's anxiety is extreme, and back when we were being helped by the best Autism specialist I've ever spoken to (and there have been a lot!), it wasn't possible for her to attend the sessions herself because of the significant and debilitating anxiety going out and seeing other people caused her. Luckily, this particular specialist understood the struggles she faced, and six months of sessions were set up with me attending on my own and speaking on behalf of my daughter. Every session I would be asked questions about how she was, and felt, and how she might respond in certain situations. The specialist would ask me what I was most concerned about, and after telling her, she would proceed to give me ideas and strategies to try and help ease the stress and make everyday things less challenging. It was incredibly refreshing to speak to someone who really understood how difficult it was for us, and some of the insights I gained definitely helped us move forward.

It wasn't long before I was sat opposite her in what would be our last session and after the usual rotation of questions and answers, the conversation eased into a more personal one. She told me that she had been studying Autism in girls and women for over thirty years, and how she wanted to thank me for helping her as much as she had helped me. I talked about the things that I had gained, and thanked her for being so compassionate as a lot of the help I had encountered over the years had been distinctly lacking that element. Then, there was a brief but extended silence in which she looked directly at me and smiled. She tilted her head to one side, and said:

"Forgive me for asking but, you do know, don't you?"

I looked at her, still silent for a minute, and then answered:

"Well... Yes. I mean, I thought it was likely, and I've thought about it since my son was diagnosed, but I've never actually had it confirmed."

She was still smiling as she spoke again:

"I've been doing this a long time, and if I was to write a description that defined the characteristics and traits of a typically Autistic woman, it would be as if I was writing about you. You tick every single classic Autism behaviour box, and it's been fascinating talking with you every session. There is absolutely no doubt that you have Autism, and I'm glad that you knew yourself before I mentioned it. I want to thank you for teaching me even more about what it is to be a woman with Autism, it's been incredibly interesting and an absolute pleasure."

We ended our conversation a few minutes after that, and I left. Walking out of her office that day I felt weirdly comforted. What she said wasn't news to me really. I had long believed that I was Autistic, not only because of the fact that all four of my children were diagnosed and there is a lot of evidence that supports Autism as being a hereditary condition (although obviously that isn't always the case), but also because I'd had to learn a lot to help my children, I had recognised most of the difficulties and patterns of behaviour, in myself.

Being told by a professional that what I had long suspected was true, was like a weight being lifted from my shoulders. It was a weight I didn't even know I had been carrying, but suddenly knowing for sure that some of the aspects of life that I had always found incredibly difficult were as a result of Autism, gave me comfort. It all made perfect sense, and for the first time ever, I felt like I had a real and true understanding why I had always had to find different ways to live my life in order to cope. Finding and accepting the coping strategies I needed to use in order to navigate life with more ease was essential and necessary, but knowing *why* I had been forced to do that, felt both reassuring and comforting. It was as if someone had given my soul a gift, and one that would help me to better nurture, understand and accept myself now and in the future.

When I got home, I immediately phoned my Mum and relayed the mornings events to her. She wasn't surprised either, and once more we spoke about all those times she had taken me to the doctor telling them that something wasn't quite right. We both had our answer now, and at the age of thirty-nine, I became the head of a very exclusive family club, who's wonderful, talented and beautiful members all lived under one roof; some of us like Jaffa Cakes and some of us don't. Actually, that's a bad example because it's not true, we all do! Let's use ice cream...some of us like it, and some of us don't, but all of it is ok.

Even though many might say we have accepted a label that now defines us, I would argue differently. We have been told why we experience the world in the way we do, and understanding that means we each get to choose how we show up and move forward. Not only that, but we get to do that without thinking that we need to fit into a mould that isn't made for us, and *that* is extremely soothing. Having a diagnosis doesn't stop us from doing anything! Having Autism or any related condition, doesn't stop us doing anything either. Instead, we get to decide what *feels* good, and… what doesn't. We get to choose whether to push ourselves out of our comfort zones or not, depending on how we feel at the time. No restrictions, no limitations, only explanations and understanding of what is, or might be possible for us.

What does Autism feel like for me? Well, it feels raw and gentle; complicated and yet incredibly simple too. I notice everything, especially the tiny things that a lot of people don't. I notice minuscule shifts in behaviour as soon as they happen and I can feel the difference in someone's demeanour long before I can understand what it is they are trying to say. I like my music extra loud so that it drowns out any other thought in my head that's trying to force its way through. But I will shrink and crumble inside if the monotonous buzz in a room full of people becomes overbearing and constant, which it almost always does. If you tell me something, I'll believe you unless you give me reason not to, in which case I will never trust you again no matter what you do to try and rebuild that trust. I dive deeply into that which I'm interested in, and become fully submerged in all its details. Some of these special interests have been constant throughout my life so far, while others come and fall away. But each one reflects a different area of my personality, and is never fully cast aside. I enjoy solitude, and find it easy compared to the distinct challenges that socialising brings with it. I'm happy in a group no bigger than three or maybe four people as long as I know them well, but larger groups (even those consisting of friends and family) are notoriously difficult and exhausting for me. In those situations, I find myself analysing every word that comes out of my mouth and those that fall from the mouths of others. There is no space in situations like that to take time, and process the information that is hurtling towards me, and I often find it completely overwhelming. Autism gifted me a resting bitch face, and just for good measure, it added in a "no filter" guarantee which again, makes experiences with little time to process information tricky. If I like you, I like you, but if I don't, I can't pretend and soon enough without me saying anything at all, you're going to work it out!

There's so much to say I can't think of it all. It's too much to try and express. But, though sometimes it can feel like I'm sinking deep into

132

soft, peaty mud that sticks to my skin, smothers me and wants to take me as its own, I also feel the soft, nurturing, warmth of that mud, enveloping my cold body and reminding me that I can't be swallowed by something that is part of the essence of my soul. Like I said, raw and gentle; complicated and simple.

I believe that my children chose me in this lifetime because their souls knew that I could understand them. They knew me before they arrived earth-side, and saw that I have lived my own life this time round from the same perspective. Seeing their difficulties from the inside, because I have those difficulties on *my* inside too, has made it easier to understand and help them. If learning for myself the hard way, was what I had to encounter in order to nurture them, then every solitary fraction of time has been worth it. Labels of any nature are often reviled in today's society, and those of us who have chosen to use them are often criticised (*especially* in the spiritual community- oh the irony) but sometimes, we need a label to help us find out what the missing ingredient is, and occasionally, when we do, it enables us to identify the exquisite and unique taste that we have been trying to pinpoint all along. The question is not how we learn to live inside the box that society deems we should fit into, but more how we learn and understand ourselves so that we feel happy living *outside* of it.

Not Normal Things #5
Meet You by The Ice Cream Van?
Part 2

It is scientifically proven that for those of us who have Autism, our brains don't work in the same way as for those who don't. It's obvious that our thought patterns and the way we process information is unusual, and whilst there is nothing "wrong" with us, the differences we are faced with quite often mean that it can sometimes feel that way, especially if we haven't learnt to embrace all of our uniqueness. For me and my children it has been a long process, and one that I'm sure will still have its trials and tribulations to overcome, but at our core we are all very sure of one thing; some of our most precious abilities and gifts, are available to us *because* of our Autism. For example; my eldest daughter's ridiculous talent for art, my eldest sons intensely compassionate nature and knowledge of anything Star Wars or car-related, my youngest son's fast processing speed and incredible gaming skills, and my youngest daughter's over-exuberant nature and ridiculously good memory are all down in part to the fact that they have Autism, and have the tenacity and mindset to become amazing at these things.

There are also hundreds of online articles, blogs and videos about the hypothetical links between Autism and spirituality-based abilities. Whether it's psychic gifts, healing ability, or topics such as Starseeds, Indigo children or more, you can find it all linked to Autism if you look in the right places.

It is believed that Star Seeds, for example, are a group of beings who were not created on Earth, and at the end of this period of awakening, will return to their home. Most Star Seeds are humans from the future that have chosen to incarnate here on Earth at this time, carrying out special missions for the benefit of Earth and humanity. These Star Seeds in particular are said to be from higher frequential dimensions or timelines, and have been known to have particular problems with adopting or coping with life on Earth. They develop specific problems related to intercommunication that include complications such as Autism, and other lifelong, similar diagnoses. Although they are sometimes extremely intelligent and often have special skills, they have a problem dealing with the sort of subjects that are taught on Earth. This theory would certainly explain some of the sensory and communication problems that people with Autism suffer from, and whilst it may seem a bit "out there" I can't say that I dismiss it entirely.

There are many similar theories such as the Star Seed concept, and none are scantily presented but are instead often written by Professors or well-educated and heavily informed intellectuals. This makes any intention to dismiss them more difficult, and as someone with an extensive knowledge and understanding of Autism *and* a deep connection to Source, it gives me some comfort thinking that these theories *could* be reality.

Even after a significant amount of research and with the understanding I have, I don't know exactly how the links work, but as an adult woman, having Autism has taught me to be more open-minded, and that is something that anyone who wants any kind of connection with spirit must be. Most of all, what's important is that you believe and trust in what works for you. After all, it really doesn't matter what anyone else thinks anyway; it's not them that have to find different ways, strategies and coping mechanisms to live their everyday life by.

Has my Autism given me my deep connection to spirit and the ability to communicate with that or those which others think they can't? I don't know is the honest answer, and I never will, but it *is* possible, just as it is for my children. I can only base my opinions on facts and my own intuition, and the rest is neither important, or necessary in this context. What I *do* know is that myself and all of my children have Autism, that is a fact along with one other undeniable truth which is that we all have some type of psychic, healing or otherwise esoteric gift. I could go into great detail about those gifts, but it won't prove or disprove the theory one way or another so there seems little point other than to show you how incredible they all are, so I won't. However, there is one strange and beautiful story which involves my youngest daughter, and most definitely has some significance and bearing on this topic of conversation.

As I have already stated in Part 1, my youngest daughter has severe anxiety. She suffers from it to a degree that would be impossible for me to make you fully comprehend, but when I tell you that it crippled her in every day of her life until more recent times, I am not exaggerating. To give you a very small amount of context, some years ago when my daughter was approximately four years old, I was told by a well experienced mental health specialist (who came to see my daughter at home), that she had never seen or come across another child whose anxiety was as severe and all-encompassing as my daughters, in her entire career. When I asked her what she could do to try and help us, she replied;

"There is nothing we can do. We have absolutely no idea how to help you I'm afraid."

Just think about that for a minute. Try and imagine just how bad a child's anxiety would have to be for someone who had been in the mental health industry for thirty or more years, and had seen thousands and thousands of children, to say that to you. I'm not sure you can, but let me tell you it was heart-breaking to watch and be part of, and terrifying to have no idea how or if, it would ever get any better.

My daughter started talking at a year old. I'm not showing off, you need to know as it's relevant. She started saying long words before she was one, and by the time she was half way through her second year, you could have a full conversation with her. Her sentences weren't even basic, they were clever and complex, and her intelligence was obvious to anyone who met her. We were always together and I would talk to her about all sorts of things, but one day when she was almost three, we had a conversation that completely blew my mind.

We were at home just doing normal things when she suddenly started sobbing. It was the sort of crying that comes from the soul, and I knew something big was really worrying her. I pulled her onto my knee and cradled her in my arms, rocking her gently as I tried to comfort her and ease her fears, but it didn't work. With her tiny nose running, and through desperate sobs, she gasped that she was scared of losing me again. I told her I wasn't going anywhere, and then asked her what she meant by "again". I told her that we hadn't ever been separated, and that no matter what happened, I would always be with her. Still sobbing, she told me that I didn't understand, and it was at that point that she became uncontrollably distressed. I did all the things that usually helped to calm her, and she settled slightly, but it was obvious that she was incredibly scared, so I gently asked her to tell me what was wrong.

With her snow coloured hands grasping on to me tightly, and her big blue eyes still struggling to contain the sheer volume of tears and fear held within them, she told me a story about herself. She told me how she had been searching for me across her last four lifetimes. She told me how her "other mothers" weren't very nice to her and how she was terrified that now she had finally found me, she might lose me again. She told me in great detail about the mother before me who had locked her in a cupboard and shouted at her constantly. She told me her name, and what she looked like and what clothes she wore. Then she told me about the one before that who would beat her repeatedly every time she spoke. She told me how the two before those weren't quite as bad, but that they ignored her and she was never good enough; how they always shouted at her for doing things wrong even when she hadn't, and how she had never been cuddled. She sobbed and held me tightly as she relayed and relived every detail of her past four lives, and I sobbed with her. As she finished telling me her darkest fears from past lifetimes that obviously still felt very real, I drew her as close to me as I could and stroked her bright blonde hair. We sat there for an hour, holding on to each other while I rocked her back and forwards and reassured her. I told her that I was so happy that she had found me, and that I would never leave her again; not ever. Her sobs eased to a soft whimper, and as she looked up at me, she asked me to promise; so, I did.

Over the next couple of years, she would often become upset and run to me with the all too familiar look of fear in her eyes. I would cuddle her while she would once more recount her past life stories to me and every time, she would ask me to promise that I would always stay with her, and every time, I did. I promised her that across all of our lifetimes, and any distance of space and time, we would be together.

As time moved on and she grew older, between us we managed little by little to get a small grip on her anxiety and her life became less stressful (although the level of stress that it is at even now, is more than most people ever experience). She will leave me for short periods, and is more than happy to stay at home with her brothers and sister while I am out. But she still holds the fear of losing me deep in her soul, and I'm not sure whether (after the hundreds of different healing modalities we have already tried) it will ever leave her. She is nine years old now, and we share a bedroom because she can't sleep without knowing I am there, and every night as I tuck her into bed, she says the same thing:

"See you in our dreams Mumma… meet you at the ice cream van?"

Of course, I reply with a resounding yes, and only then does she roll over and happily fall into sleep.

The level of fear due to this, that my daughter had been carrying with her and to some extent still is, must have been phenomenal. I can't comprehend how frightening knowing, feeling and reliving these truths, that were still crystal clear in her consciousness after hundreds of years, must have been. So is it any wonder that she had such severe anxiety?! Is it possible that a child who is not even three years old can bear witness to something such as this? Yes, it is, and I would argue to the death with anyone who tried to tell me that what she told me that day and the many times since, was just a figment of her imagination. The details were too precise and the sheer terror that she felt is not something one gets from some crazy, imaginative journey. *It is her reality*, and it demonstrates the link between physical manifestation and spiritual capability. I'm not saying that all of her anxiety is caused by what she has remembered from previous lifetimes, but it most certainly is a factor and one that can't and shouldn't, be ignored. Furthermore, if her anxiety is a symptom of her Autism as we have been told, and the memories are a manifestation of that anxiety, isn't it at least possible that her ability to remember those things in the first place, could be in part, due to her having Autism?

This example also backs up the belief that I have always held around souls choosing their parents before conception. My own daughter told me that she had been trying to find me for hundreds of years, and she told me this at an age that she wouldn't have ever heard of that theory at any point in her little life. Not that this has any bearing on the Autism conversation, but I believe it is worth mentioning while it's in context.

I suppose, as always, I can only really speak for myself, and within the boundaries of that constraint there are sureties that speak for themselves. Of course, these certainties of mine are aided by the fact that I don't believe in coincidence at all. Everything that appears as a coincidence is in fact synchronicity, and on that basis, the nature of my own thoughts around whether there is a link between Autism and spirituality can only be seen as a definite thumbs up.

Many people, including myself, would describe me as a bit different. I've been called a weirdo in both jest and a more bullying way, many times over, and neither bother me. Is my unusual nature a symptom of my Autism as many would argue, or am I seen as weird because I can do the things I do? What I am certain of is that having Autism has made me more resilient. I have had to find ways to cope in a society that doesn't like anyone who doesn't fit neatly into a box.

That has been hard, but eventually it also enabled me to have the strength to be myself no matter what, and that is a priceless lesson. Being Autistic has given me a unique view of the world. There are so many things in life that I notice that others never have, and never will, and whilst the filter that Autism puts on everything can be overwhelmingly challenging, it has also gifted me the opportunity to see things in a unique way. My perception of what is possible for all of us, is not just moulded by the Not Normal Things that fill these pages and my amazing connection to Source, but also by the neurodiverse glasses that I look through every day and can't ever take off. Would I change it for myself if I could? That's easy to answer: no, I wouldn't. I like my over-exaggerated facial expressions that come from years of watching and copying how other people interact with each other. I'm fond of my excruciatingly literal brain and how its interpretation of conversations means I sometimes say things that bring about copious amounts of laughter for those involved. I love that I'm a geek when it comes to my special interests, and that I never know when a new, temporary one is going to arrive and engage me in a frenzy of fresh discovery and knowledge. I've grown into my Autism, but I've had the luxury of doing that alongside four other humans that chose me to guide them in their own journey, and that has and always will be a blessing that I'm grateful for, and a privilege that I will never take for granted.

I'm as certain as I can be that there aren't any ice cream vans in the next dimension, but somehow, between the stubborn rigidity of thinking that Autism bestows on us, the abilities we have all been graciously gifted, and the liberal sprinkling of Magick that fills our everyday lives, I'm sure that we will all find the energetic space that one might occupy, and when the time comes, that's exactly where I'll be waiting.

P.S.

Within the judgement of others is a failing of space for compassion, and an innate lack of understanding. All of us, have at some time judged someone else for something, but throughout my full experience of Autism which has incorporated all genders, ages and differences, I have witnessed some shocking acts of intolerance.

If you have been looking at spiritual wellbeing for any length of time, you will have no doubt come across the theory that every time we judge someone else, we are judging an unhealed part of ourselves. Whilst this is true, it doesn't show people *how* to overcome falling into the trap of judging others, and neither does it help them to recognise what it is they are unhealed from.

I have spent a lot of time looking at this area for myself in the last ten years, and I believe that the key to releasing judgement, is found by working on two things.

Compassion is something we are all capable of. There are some who aren't as open to the gentle and loving energy that comes with an air of compassion, and they often shy away from it without even realising they're doing so, which can lead them to harshly judge other people. Some people are extremely compassionate and can become *so* overwhelmed by the emotions they feel, that they *then* start to judge the ones who aren't showing as much compassion to others as they would like or expect. As with everything in life, moderation is key. That doesn't mean that you have to put a lid on the amount of compassion you feel, or conversely, start forcing yourself to show more. It means that whatever your true nature wants to feel and do is right, *but* that you must temper that with understanding for the situation of others.

If there are people who seem to be bullying a section of society, or showing a general lack of compassion, it's not for you to try and force them into doing the opposite, but to have understanding about why they behave that way *even though* it isn't in line with your own beliefs. Trying to understand why other people act in the way they do, and show enough compassion to accept that there might be a reason for their behaviour that you're not aware of, is the recipe that facilitates the release of judgement within yourself, and enables you to start working out why you might have judged them in the first place.

Learning about Autism and the way it can manifest, especially in children, made me much more open and compassionate about allowing that space for others, whether they needed it or not. We've all seen and heard a small child screaming at the top of their voice in a supermarket, and maybe even throwing themselves on the floor, and even I have at some point in the past, made some kind of judgment about that kind of behaviour. But none of us know what is going on in a stranger's life, or whether there are issues surrounding that child or family that might explain why it was happening, so can't we extend some compassion and maybe even try and understand?

Once you stop jumping on the judgement treadmill and mindfully walk in your own lane (and allow others to walk in theirs), it's amazing how much more peace flows through you. Even the way you show up for yourself is positively affected, and along with that, once those around you notice (even if it's on a subconscious level) *they* will feel able to truly show up as themselves because they know you will accept them no matter what. Dropping the need to judge, gives yourself and those around you real freedom.

Of course, there will always be those who haven't learnt this lesson yet, and whilst it might be tempting to judge them for that, if you do, you are only feeding back in to the machine that you have otherwise worked to escape from. Instead, try and educate them on the things they feel the need to criticise so harshly, and do it without expectation of change and from a place of compassion too. That's all you can do and as the old saying goes, you can lead a horse to water but you can't make it drink. Standing and shouting at it is certainly not going to work! I like to think that in cases such as this, if you lead the horse to water, give it all the tools it needs to make an educated choice and grant it the space to make wise and loving decisions for itself, the chances of it quenching its thirst are much ameliorated.

Judgement pops up everywhere, so I ask you to look at your life today, and see if there is anything you can release judgement around; that could be anything and the subject may even surprise you. Whatever it is, try and show some compassion and embrace some level of understanding, and then you can begin to show up in a more graceful and loving way to everyone, including yourself.

Not Normal Things #6
Always Bet on The Worm
Part 1

I thought I was a really strong woman. I'd been through some pretty difficult stuff in my life when I reached the age of thirty-six, and having navigated my not so friendly divorce (it was definitely *not* a conscious uncoupling) and setting myself and the children up in a new home, deceptively lured me into the illusion that I had all my ducks in a pretty little row. Holy shit, how wrong I was.

When I left our marital home, I left with the children, their belongings, my belongings and their beds. With the exception of a couple of bits of furniture that were family heirlooms, such as the 1960's dressing table my mum gave me, and an old chest of drawers, I left almost everything else behind in a desperate bid to just get out of the situation. So, when we moved into our new home in the same town, I more or less had to start again. I brought second hand sofas, a new-to-me bed for myself, and filled the house with items salvaged from skips and charity shops. I have always had a knack for doing up old furniture and making it look amazing, and skip diving (with permission of course) is also a talent that I've been happy to utilise. That's exactly what I did, and with hard work, bit by bit, I was creating a lovely home for the children and myself.

We lived in a very grand house that I had manifested; truly, it's an amazing manifestation story, although is also a great example of how sometimes what you call in doesn't always arrive looking the way you expect it to. In my case, and this instance, it (the house I'd manifested *years* before) arrived as a result of the breakdown of my marriage, which I certainly wouldn't have imagined at the time I set the intention to live there, but I got what I'd asked for and as new beginnings go, that house was a really lovely place to start one.

After the dust settled, we were well on our way to recovering from what had obviously been an extremely turbulent and emotionally harrowing time. I was beginning to find myself again and enjoyed the freedom of being able to do whatever I wanted within my own space. I could listen to whatever music I wanted, cook what I wanted, watch what I wanted and do all of those things whenever I wanted to. The freedom of being able to do those things was a much welcomed positive in a situation that had been rife with so much negativity, and I relished them all.

For the first time in my life, I bought myself a brand-new car on a payment plan from the local Peugeot garage; it was electric blue with white ears (wing mirrors) and I absolutely loved it! I even managed to treat myself to a brand spanking new Notebook (like a small laptop). Things were good, and even though I was still wading through the emotional fallout from what had happened, I felt like I was adjusting really well and recovering quickly. Of course, at this time I wasn't into spiritual and mental wellbeing like I am now, so I had no idea that many of the traumas from the things that had happened in my first marriage were sitting quietly within me, and would come to be the very things that facilitated an even more devastating and destructive one.

Looking after the children was my first priority, and after a few months had passed we all seemed happier than we had been for years. Having the time to strengthen my relationship with them had been a wonderful gift, and although we had always shown as much love to each other as any other loving parent/child relationship does, somehow, we seemed closer than ever and had a bond that was unrivalled by anyone or anything. It was beautiful, and whilst it was born out of extremely difficult circumstances, I was incredibly grateful that we had been given the opportunity to discover a deeper connection and way of being, together.

I did find myself feeling lonely though, and whilst, if I felt that way now, I would most definitely pay closer attention to those feelings and unpick them, back then I didn't even know that I *should* have been doing that, let alone how to. I spoke to the children about how I felt, and about dating again, and they said that all they wanted was for me to be happy, so I did what most people do, and searched for someone to fill the gaps within myself. My eldest son told me to consider online dating, so I decided to dip my toe in what were, for me, the very unchartered waters of the internet, to see what happened.

As anyone who has entered the world of internet dating before will tell you, there are always an abundance of very odd people who find their way into your inbox (I particularly remember the Giant Haystacks lookalike in the orange prison boiler-suit who thought a great way to get me to reply to him was to send a message saying simply "message me back now"), but along with the unsavoury people, there were people who seemed genuinely nice, and it wasn't too long until I met someone who seemed to fit into that group.

The details around how it all happened aren't really important so, in short, we met, we got on, and we started seeing each other. It all happened very quickly, much too quickly in fact, and whilst I see that now, at the time I was relishing in the attention and complements I was suddenly getting after having been lacking in them for many years, so ignored the ridiculous speed at which it was going at.

When you have spent a really long time feeling unloved and unwanted, it feels amazing when someone starts to tell you nice things about yourself. Having spent at least the last seven years in the barren wasteland of my marriage, finding someone who was telling me incredible and wonderful things was almost like a drug. I started to feel like I was someone who was worthy of being loved, and more than that, like being in a loving relationship was actually possible. I was being completely swept off my feet, and whilst it almost felt too good to be true, I clung to the fact that this time, things might just turn out to be amazing.

Having said that, even right at the beginning of whatever it was we were starting, there were tiny moments when I would feel uneasy about something he did or said, but I paid no attention to them and pushed forward trying only to feel the good stuff. I convinced myself that those "uncomfortable for a reason I wasn't sure of" moments were due to trust issues I had from the past, and that over time I would get over them and wouldn't have to worry about them anymore. I had friends who had met him, and didn't like him for no logical reason they could give. But I ignored them too and chose to trust my own instincts, which in reality meant I was listening to the false instincts that I had created to fit into my agenda, and forced my true ones into silence. Did I want or ask for what was about to come and turn my life upside down? No, most certainly not, but there is absolutely no doubt that all the warning signs were there and I was too vulnerable, too scared of being alone, and inextricably lacking in self-awareness to heed them.

After a really short period of time, it became obvious to me that he was at the house more and more. He told me his house was being renovated and was almost uninhabitable with no flooring, no heating and no bathroom. I felt guilty sending him home to that, so I let him stay. He had just been made redundant too, and spent most of the day at my house looking for work using my Notebook. Without any real discussion, or passing of any amount of time, it seemed we were living together and whilst I felt uneasy about it, it was also nice, and I didn't feel able to tell him that it was too soon because of the difficult circumstances he found himself in, so I kept quiet.

I had always found myself wanting to care for and help people who were in need or broken. I could feel their pain before anything else, and even in my thirties I hadn't worked out that this wasn't just a part of my personality, but a gift from my soul that could, if misunderstood, and left unprotected by me, make it incredibly easy for other people to prey on. Nowadays there's loads of information about what it means to be an Empath, and a wealth of lessons about how to ensure that you don't fall into the common traps that many Empaths do. But ten years ago, despite knowing what I did about Spirit, Tarot and many other aspects of the occult, I didn't even know anything about it or even that I was one, and this left me wide open to all kinds of mistreatment. I suppose that *something* had to finally wake me up, and if the dark path that my life was about to turn down wasn't enough to do so, then I don't think anything would have been.

I had noticed even in the short time we had been together that he liked things to be done a certain way, and if they weren't, he would become moody. It only happened in relation to small things at first, and certainly not in any way that made me worry, but it was noticeable. He didn't like the lemonade in the fridge and would take any bottle that I put in there out, even though I had said that I preferred it cold. If he couldn't find something, he would blame someone else for moving it and become cross until he, or someone else, found it. Small things, and silly things, but things that changed the otherwise happy and calm atmosphere of the house. One day, whilst he was still out of work, he offered to take my card and do my weekly food shop while I was at work. I wasn't sure so said that I would do it. He became moody and said he was only trying to help, so I agreed as it would save me a lot of time and I didn't want to cause an argument. I gave him my cash card and pin, and went to work as usual.

I got home from work later that day to find him sat at the kitchen table looking very agitated. He couldn't sit still and seemed really anxious. I asked him if everything was ok, and he told me that he was nervous because he had done something nice as a surprise and was worried that I would be upset about it. I sat down at the table and told him to tell me what it was. He was totally wired, and I had no idea what to expect.

In the ten minutes that followed, he told me that he had wanted to do something special for me, and had booked a surprise holiday to South Africa where we would go on safari. I was gobsmacked and whilst I wanted to be excited, I knew the conversation wasn't over yet, and waited nervously to see what else he had to say. He said that he had booked it that day at the travel agents, and whilst he was going to pay for it all, he had had to pay a deposit there and then so had used my money to do it. The deposit was five hundred pounds and had almost cleared out my bank account, but he said it was ok because I'd have it back in the next couple of days as he was waiting for money to clear in his account.

I don't know if you've ever felt excited about something someone was telling you and pissed off at the same time, but it's extremely confusing. On top of that, he was sat in front of me telling me that he had come up with this amazing idea and wanted me to experience something incredible after having come through such a difficult time, and that the money I had spent (without actually agreeing to) would be returned to me by the end of the week. I was angry, but I'm not generally an angry person and my default position is usually one of understanding and compassion, so I said it was ok and that it was a lovely thing for him to have thought about, despite the way he went about it. He spent the next hour or so showing me the holiday details online, and no one could have argued that it wasn't spectacular.

I went to bed that evening with a weird feeling in my stomach. I wanted to be happy, but I just couldn't shake the feeling that something was seriously wrong. But it was too late now; it had been done, and at least I would have the money back in my account soon and the bills that it was meant for would swallow it up as usual, and everything would be back on an even keel.

The end of the week came and went but my money didn't. It was still MIA although I was promised that it was on the way. I believed him – I had no reason not to, so I waited.

In the weeks that passed after that, I was told of the unfortunate circumstances that meant I wouldn't be able to get my five hundred pounds back any time soon, and as a result, I asked if we could cancel the holiday and get the deposit back. The obvious answer to that question was no of course, as that's exactly the meaning of a deposit in the first place, but it was worth a try. I felt bad that he felt so sorry and embarrassed about it all, so I didn't make a big deal out of it and made a million phone calls to spread the missed bills out so that everything was back to running smoothly again, and that was that.

Time passed, and with it went Friday after Friday of him doing my weekly shop. I often wondered how it took someone so long to do a small amount of shopping, and how such a little amount of shopping cost more and more, but not to the point where there was any evidence that something was seriously wrong. My confidence still hadn't been restored after what happened with my first husband, and I still doubted myself a lot which made speaking out feel difficult. By this time, there were really small things were being said and done that I felt a little confused about, but again, didn't feel were big enough to mention. There were more of the "uncomfortable" feelings that I'd had at the very beginning, but they seemed to be getting bigger and much harder to ignore as a result, so despite not voicing them, I had no choice but to start listening to them at least. It was clear that *something* was amiss, but I just didn't quite know what, and I was unsure how to find out too.

Then things started to go missing. Little things but expensive things, and most of them were completely unexplainable. I had bought iPods for the children the first Christmas after we got back on our feet, and they treasured them. They each had a different coloured one, and they looked after them meticulously. My house was a tidy and organised one too, so when they went missing from their usual resting place it was odd and we couldn't work out how. We searched everywhere, but we just couldn't find them. The toy box that was their usual home when not being used, was also searched, but they were nowhere to be seen.

A month later after having been gone for ages one Saturday morning when we had visitors, he came back in and disappeared into the house. Me and our visitors (who were very old friends of mine), were in the kitchen chatting when, ten minutes after having walked in, he called me into the room where the toy box was. He announced loudly and happily in front of everyone, that he had found the iPods! He had been looking for something and dropped it down the back against the wall, and when he went to retrieve it, the iPods were there! *I knew they hadn't been under there.* I had moved every item of furniture in the house to look for them, and *I absolutely knew* they weren't there. I didn't know what to say, and was embarrassed as the whole display seemed over-the-top and exaggerated, but I wasn't about to say anything in front of my friends, so acted pleased and carried on as normal.

That was the first time I realised that unwittingly and totally subconsciously, I had started to hide some of the unexplainable things that had started to happen more and more frequently, from my friends and family. It felt alien to me to pull away and keep things hidden, as I had always been an open book and was very close to those around me, but there was no way I could tell them some of the strange things that were happening as they wouldn't understand why I hadn't spoken out about them, and admitting that I felt afraid to do so would only worry them and compound my own confusion further. So, I kept my concerns to myself and tried to stop it from swirling around in my head too much. That day was also the first time that I realised that I was scared of him. I don't mean a little bit scared either; I was *really fucking scared* of him and what his response might be to anything I did or said. Worse still, I didn't know what to do about it.

Even writing as little as I have about what was starting to unfold back then, brings back the thoughts that I am, and was, stupid and pathetic. I'm inherently aware that for most people, the alarm bells would be sounding so fucking loudly by this point that there would be no way things would have been left to continue in the same way. But what you may not see or understand is that it was very different being *in it*, even at this stage. I was still being told amazing things and paid lots of attention to, which felt as new as it had the few months before. I was given gifts at unexpected moments, and that was something I had never experienced before either. Those things all felt really good. Even the oddest occurrences of money going missing, or being less than expected, had some sort of explanation in the end, and above all, I *wanted* to see the positives. I wanted everything to be ok and I was starting to believe (with a gentle nudge in the right direction from him) that anything I did bring up, was all in my head. I was, despite my own delusions about my strength of character at the time, really fucking vulnerable. As sad and difficult as that is for me to admit even after all these years, I couldn't see the bad in him that others did. I didn't see what was coming because I was incredibly naive and being led to believe something entirely different than the truth. When someone is vulnerable, it's easy for anyone who really wants to, to manipulate them into believing just about anything. On top of that, when you are being encouraged by any means possible to look in a different direction, it's incredibly easy to completely miss something that's right in front of you. Despite my very real fear and my misgivings about the path we were treading, I was in way over my head and I thought that whatever happened, good or bad, it would be ok in the end. So, I carried on.

Over the short period of a few weeks, more things went missing and those items started to be more important and significant things too. My wedding and engagement ring from my first marriage disappeared, both of which I was saving to give to my daughter one day. They were platinum, and my engagement ring had been hand-made with diamonds and aqua marine. Both were worth a lot of money, but more significantly, were pretty much the only thing of any real value (sentimental and monetary) that I had to pass down to my children. I didn't need to search for them as I kept them in a specific place that I thought only I knew about…obviously, I was wrong.

He started working for his Mum, and asked if he could borrow my Notebook as he needed it at work. I didn't see it again for weeks. I kept asking if he could bring it home as I needed it, but he kept forgetting.

Money went missing out of my purse almost daily. My cash card would go missing and my bank account would be depleted soon after.

The iPods went several times and came back again. As did anything else of any remote value; jewellery left to me by my nan, or given to me by my Mum, even a TV once. For the things I dared challenge him about, there was always an excuse; it had broken and he'd taken it to be mended, or he was having it cleaned as a surprise, or he had borrowed it for a friend. Something… anything…there was always a reason, and that made it extremely difficult to do anything about. It didn't matter what I said, he *never* backed down, and it would be turned around to appear that it was *me* who was in the wrong. *I* was the one who was making things up, not him. He would get really angry and aggressive and storm out of the house, shouting abuse at me and slamming doors behind him leaving me feeling scared, worried and completely at a loss as to what to do. I felt like I was actually going mad and didn't know what to believe. I was gaslighted a million times a day, and I just couldn't gain enough clarity to see it. Everything became a kind of blur but it was only just the beginning.

It wasn't much long however, before the truth came out, and it didn't happen in the way I expected either. I thought I'd find out one way or another, but as it happens, he straight up told me.

I went to work like I did every day after dropping the children at school. I did my work, talked to friends, and generally had a most unremarkable day. Until I got home.

I walked in the door of my house and he wasn't there. I text to say I was home and he replied saying he wasn't coming back. There was no warning, no reason, just a message saying he couldn't come back and he was sorry. Of course, I rang but he didn't answer. He sent me another message telling me that he was no good for me, and that I was better off without him. I asked him what he was talking about and said he should just come back home so that we could talk about whatever it was that was going on, properly. Eventually, after more self-deprecating texts, he agreed, and soon after he was stood opposite me in the hallway.

His head was hung low, and he leant against the wall and slid down it until he was sitting on the floor with his knees bent. I sat down next to him and asked him what had happened. He looked at me, and told me that that afternoon, while I was at work, he had been to the bank and withdrawn every single penny that was in my account. It was payday. He continued to tell me that he had taken the eleven hundred pounds that I had been paid that morning, and gambled every single penny until there was nothing left.

The air was still, and completely silent for some time. I sat there next to him, and as he began to cry, I felt panic fill my head. My rent was due in two days, how was I going to pay it? How would I pay the bills for the entire month and how the fuck was I going to feed my children!? My head was spinning and I didn't know what to do. He was crying with his head in his hands, and saying he was sorry over and over. He begged me to forgive him and told me I didn't deserve what he had done, and that if I forgave him, he would get help. I just didn't have it within me to shout and scream at him, so I told him it was ok and that we would sort it out. He agreed that he would call the doctor the next day to try and access more help, and would start going to GA meetings and after a couple of hours, the conversation was over.

I was left reeling. I had absolutely no idea how I was going to pay for everything that month, but I tried really hard not to panic as I knew it wouldn't help. I would make calls the next day and see what I could sort out. He said he would call his Dad and see if he would help too, which felt like some sort of relief even though it was in no way guaranteed.

The money was a worry, especially with the children, but with the worry there was also some relief. Finally, he had admitted that he had a serious problem and for that small moment I knew it wasn't all in my head. It explained his terrible mood swings which by now, were even more aggressive and frequent, and with his promise of getting help, I felt like there was some hope at least. I shouldn't have been relieved, but I was. I should have told him out get out and never come back at that point, but I didn't. I wanted to help him get better and it felt like a huge weight had been lifted from my shoulders that it was out in the open. Now, I thought, things would start to improve.

I believe that it was at this time that my spirituality was really starting to pull me forward. Everything felt difficult, but I also had glimmers of feeling more like myself at times and that happened in the fleeting moments that I had when I wasn't scared, hurt or angry. Those tiny fragments of feeling like myself, happened when I was thinking about what to do from a place of love. I wanted more than anything to help him sort his life out and be happy. I wanted him to be free of the pain and burden I saw him in every day. I wanted to be the one who didn't walk away and leave because it got difficult, and although it was all intrinsically misguided, somewhat ego-led and remarkably naive, all of it came from the purest of intentions. True to Empath-style form, and in conjunction with the most loving and gentle parts of my personality, I decided I had to make it work, no matter what. That decision would turn out to be both the best, and the worst decision I would ever make.

The next week felt happier. He had found a GA meeting to go to on a Wednesday evening and I had real hope that he might genuinely get better. I did a load of research about addicts, in particular gambling addicts, and whilst it was terrifying to read some of the stories I did, it also made me feel less alone. He and I talked in depth about his addiction and I started to understand it more. It was incredibly sad to hear some of the things he told me, and the pain and havoc it had so far caused on his life was glaringly obvious.

I had two really close friends at this time who I had spent a lot of time with and known since I moved to the area, and I reluctantly confided some of what had happened, to them. That too felt like a relief at first, but they were desperate for me to leave him, and I felt under a huge amount of pressure to do just that when I didn't feel able to. It was in one of these conversations with them both urging me to leave him that I broke down and told them I couldn't, because I had just discovered that I was pregnant.

It was as if I was living two lives and neither of them felt real. In one I was desperately unhappy and couldn't wait to leave and start again away from the verbal abuse, anger, aggression and huge financial strain of never knowing whether I would have enough money to pay the bills and feed the children that day. In the other, I was a supportive and loving partner to an addict, who was working full time, raising and shielding three amazing children and trying really hard to be happy and pretending everything was ok to everyone. I felt like Jekyll and Hyde, and it was exhausting. Finding out I was pregnant was a joy despite it all though, I could never say otherwise, and I truly believed that him finding out he was going to be a Father would make him realise that he needed to turn his life around. When I told him, he said exactly that, and for a few hours, the confusion eased a little again. I should have known that it wouldn't last long, but what I couldn't have foreseen is that things were about to get much, much worse.

Not Normal Things #6
Always Bet on The Worm
Part 2

After a very brief period of abstinence from gambling (maybe a couple of weeks tops), he soon fell back into old habits and everything was a mess again. This time though, I was carrying our baby.

There were too many times to mention where stuff went missing or cash was taken; it happened almost daily. In the space of the few months since I fell pregnant, my Notebook had gone completely never to be seen again, I had lost my car as I no longer had the money I needed to make the final bubble payment so had to hand it back, and had been forced to move out from the house I lived in as the owners wanted to sell it and despite them offering to lend me the money for the deposit so I could get a mortgage for it, I knew that there was no way on earth I was financially stable enough to do so anymore. Most of my jewellery had been pawned without my consent, anything of any real value had gone with it over time too, and I was pretty much on my arse in every sense.

We moved into a house in the same town, but it was hard work to meet the rent every month, and every day was a worry as I didn't know what I was going to have to face, or what sort of mood he would be in when he got home. The children were scared of him too now as he bullied them terribly, and I think the worst thing of all was the constant yo-yoing of emotions and the fact that we were all constantly treading on eggshells.

We were all scared of him, and there had been more than one occasion when he had lashed out and thrown things. There was one time in particular when he scared the boys so badly, and hurt one of them with a bottle that he threw, that I nearly lost my shit and ended it all there and then. But I was stood at the top of the stairs next to him, and I was six months pregnant so frightened and reluctantly, I said nothing and went in to the children to make sure they were alright. I felt guilty for not standing up to him, and although once he was gone (he almost always stormed out of the house soon after an outburst) the children and I sat and cuddled on their beds, it didn't stop me feeling like the worst mother in the world. I was supposed to look after them, they meant everything to me, and here I was putting them in danger by not leaving him. It just wasn't that simple though, and I felt utterly trapped.

By this time, I had also discovered that he was "talking" to other women which made me feel even more worthless and unwanted than I had ever felt before. He tried to hide it, but not very well, and I often saw photos and messages on his phone. When I was eight months pregnant, on Valentine's Day, he sat at the other end of the sofa opposite me on his phone, without realising that there was a mirror behind him; I could read every word and see everything he was doing. He was talking to a girl on the internet telling her how beautiful she was, and how he was bored and wished he could see her right now. I was sat right there, with our child inside me almost ready to be born, and it didn't faze him for a second. It was heart-breaking, and I was beside myself with fear of what might be, and self-loathing.

I couldn't argue with him because he ran rings around me; he would say things to confuse me, and it only made matters worse. He would be in a foul mood for days and we would all be terrified of him coming through the door, so I stayed quiet because at least that way the children were less likely to get in trouble. All I had left were my beautiful children, but even at that point, I wasn't ready to end it, and it was far from over.

Everything he had told me was a lie, right from the very beginning. There had (obviously) never been a safari holiday and my five hundred pounds wasn't spent on a deposit but instead on a horse race, football match or slot machine in the bookies. He wasn't made redundant either. He had inadvertently left a letter out one day that was from his old employer saying that he was due to go in for an interview about money that had been taken from petty cash, and had been suspended pending the outcome. I asked him why he had been made redundant later, on the same day that I saw the letter, and he told me some story about something that made no real sense, but the truth was very different and that job was one of several that he had used to his advantage, and then lost as a result. I also found out that the house he was having renovated belonged to his dad and whilst it was in a total mess, and he had been staying there, it wasn't being renovated at all - he had chosen to live there as it was. There were so many lies about so many things and I no longer believed a word that came out of his mouth. But still I stayed.

Spiritual or connected people talk about The Dark Night of the Soul a lot, and whenever I read about it, it always sounds like they're talking about some shadowy, cosmic event that has come for them but that isn't linked to real life. It's not like that at all. My first real Dark Night of the Soul came about from meeting this man on the internet and following the path he led me down for the next couple of years. All of it, and I'm not done telling you about it yet, was visceral and painful, and dark, and so very fucking real. It was tangible; it was actually happening and yet it was like the worst nightmare I'd ever had. I suppose the good news is that eventually you wake up from even the worst of bad dreams, but not until you've learnt everything you need to from it.

For all the bad, there were glimmers of good too. Sadly, his actions meant that none of us trusted anything he did or said as we knew it could change on a sixpence, but he did try to do nice things. He took the children to places they wanted to go and still bought us all gifts for no reason. Again, the shine from these placations was dulled due to the fact that we all knew that the money for them almost always had been won or stolen. He had been happy to get me whatever I wanted while I was pregnant and often trawled the shops late at night when I ran out of fresh pineapple (something I couldn't live without and had been craving throughout). He was happy when he thought that we were happy, and that made things easier. I often looked at him and thought he resembled a little boy in that way; he wanted to please people, it's just that sometimes, he didn't know how. I knew he needed help, and I was determined to find new ways to do just that, but I was beginning to wonder whether I would find anything that would ever work.

Everything stopped when I went into labour. All the worry and emotional pain was put on hold and I could only concentrate on bringing my baby into the world. I had had a very difficult pregnancy health wise, and had been very poorly, so I was ready for our little girl to join us earth side no matter what lay ahead. In those terms it was an uncertain time, but give him his due, he was amazing throughout my labour and gave me everything I needed. I gave birth to our daughter and he was there with me when I did. I think she had been here about six hours before I started to panic about what he was doing, who he was with, and how the children were.

It was all so much more intricate and complex than it can ever be explained. Interwoven into all of it were larger family dynamics, friendships, work and all of the things that weave together to make life what it is. There is no way I could portray it all because I can't even remember it all. There are all the little things that compound the bigger events and make everything feel impossible, along with the several million thoughts that tore through my head every minute of every day; there were times when I thought it might explode from them all. Those thoughts were unstoppable, inescapable and for the majority of the time, pretty depressing and hopeless. I had no sense of myself anymore, and any faint slither of the person I had begun to find after my first divorce, was gone. There was no intentional spiritual practice, no self-worth, self-love or even sense of self at all, there was only survival and existence.

As I have said before, writing parts of this has brought those old feelings of shame back to the surface, and none more so than what I am about to tell you next. So much so that I considered leaving it out of the book entirely, but I not only *can't* do that, but I don't want to either. The reason this book came about in the first place was because I wanted to share my story to help other people going through the same things, so sharing my uncensored truth is the only option I have. It's also a good way of showing you just how much you can change your life around if you really want to, and that *no matter what you have chosen in the past*, the *only* thing that really matters, is *what you choose to do now*. So …

After all of this, during all of this, and knowing how I felt, and how unhappy we all were, when he proposed to me not long after our daughter was born, I said yes.

Jesus. Wtf, right? I know, really, I do. I get it. No one will ever judge me as harshly as I have judged myself about any of this, so I have nothing to be afraid of in that sense, and I don't really know what to tell you except that I thought it would help. Looking back on it now, it would be laughable if it wasn't so tragic, and I understand why people would think that it's incredibly stupid. But once again, when I was in it, it just wasn't like that, and I won't judge myself for it anymore. It was different. *I* was different. Everything was different and I was lost, frightened, lonely and desperate for something nice. He must have loved me if he wanted to get married? Maybe things would change. Maybe *this* would be the thing that made him realise what he needed to do. Maybe I would finally be enough for him; for someone.

A few months later, we went away to Gretna Green, where all good runaways go to get married, and we did just that. And even on our wedding day, after we got back to the house we were staying in, he snuck off to the library to check his seedy emails from all the girls he was looking at/talking to, and go to the bookies. Happy Days.

Getting married didn't change a thing, in fact I think it made them worse. He cleared out the bank account completely not long afterwards and we missed a rent payment as a result. We had to move out and had nowhere to go and no money either. The house that his Dad had let him stay in before, with no floor, no proper bathroom or kitchen, was empty, so he let us stay there and pay nominal rent to cover the mortgage. The floors were mended and we decorated, but the kitchen and bathroom were almost unworkable and it was an extremely difficult time. I was however, glad and grateful to have a home and the children's rooms upstairs were lovely; I had made sure of that.

I don't know if it was the situation overall, the increase in gambling since we got married, severe poverty, or the pressure of the last couple of years finally taking its toll, but I started to feel really low. In the Introduction and Not Normal Thing #1, Part 2, I mentioned waking up one day and wanting to take my own life; well this is when that happened. I was bereft and exhausted, and couldn't see a way out. I felt ashamed and embarrassed at what I had allowed and who I had become. I felt like a shitty mother who couldn't do what her children deserved and needed, and every single day was like walking through hell. He was more aggressive, more controlling, more addicted and more unpredictable than ever, and now we were in his Dad's house, I felt the walls closing in at a rate of knots that made me feel like I was being drowned in thick, hot tar. I had reached rock-bottom and there was no escape. Or at least that's what it felt like, but only twenty-four hours later, I would find a slither of hope and with a little help, uncover the battered and worn emergency exit door.

That next morning, I went to the doctors. She was the first person I told about everything and as I sat there spilling my awful life out into the open and crying uncontrollable tears, something shifted. I felt it. It was as if I'd found a key and unlocked a door that had been welded shut and hidden from view by overgrown ivy and old trees. It wasn't the moment that I knew I was going to leave, but it was the moment that my own sense of self started stretching its unused and forgotten muscles again, and ultimately, it was the beginning of my beginning.

The doctor listened and told me that I had to make changes now. She examined me, and told me that if things didn't change soon, I would have a nervous exhaustion breakdown. She explained that although I had been carrying on as normal and thought I was physically fine, my body had started to crumble under the stress, and that I was becoming extremely physically ill. She told me that, if I didn't sort my shit out, she would expect that within a couple of weeks I would collapse and have to be admitted to hospital where I would have to remain for some time. I knew I couldn't let that happen because my children would be left with him, and there was no way that was going to happen.

I went home and I set to work. Every day I spent time on forums for people and family members affected by those who gamble. It was horrifying and I realised that there were women like me who had stayed married in the vain hope that things would change, but never had. These women had lost everything, like I had, but were still trying, and still miserable. Some of them had been in this destructive cycle for thirty or forty years, and it was enough to scare me more than he did. Finally.

I started to gradually build up my confidence by joining a church group for women which I knew was a safe place, and spending as much time as I could doing things I liked when he was out of the house. I had become so controlled that I wasn't capable of writing a shopping list, so I practiced. I practiced everything that I had forgotten how to do, and gradually I started to feel better.

Whilst it was great that I was finding myself again, it meant that there was more tension between us. I was no longer so complicit, and it didn't go down well. We argued a lot, and I started to have feelings towards him that I'd never felt like hatred and anger. Every time he spoke to the children badly, I told him to stop, and also had to hold down the urge to beat the crap out of him. It was new, and it was difficult in its own way.

I shared my story with the women at the church group, and my closest friends, and they were all amazing. I felt supported in a way that I hadn't for a long time, and whilst I had lost friends along the way, I had enough around me and knew there was always someone I could turn to.

Time went by and nothing changed from his perspective apart from the fact that he knew I was tired of his games and constant bullshit. This was never more evident than the day I told him it was over, and even now his response in that moment still surprises me when I think of it.

He left for work in the morning, and as I had done every single morning for the last year or so, I did my rounds. In order to keep tabs on what he was taking, every morning I went round the house, into every room, and I checked certain things. This Not Normal Thing meant I had to adapt to and create a new way of living, and my daily check run was one of the strategies I had put in place. I always checked the children's money boxes along with jewellery boxes, trinkets, games consoles and electrical items. I had a method, and knew exactly how much was where at any given time. My youngest son, on this particular morning, should have had thirteen pounds in his money box but when I checked, it had gone.

I had come to expect to find things missing, but for some reason the theft of that thirteen pounds was so significant it felt like the earths tectonic plates had suddenly just shifted under my feet, and there was an anger rising in me that was so fierce I couldn't have quieted it if I'd wanted to. As it happens, this time I didn't want to, and as I stood in my son's bedroom looking at the empty upturned pot, I knew that I had reached my limit.

I flew down the stairs with a fire burning in my stomach, and angry, terrible, gut wrenching words flying around my head. As I've said, in the scheme of things, thirteen pounds was nothing, and in comparison to the *thousands and thousands* he had taken before, it seemed odd that all of a sudden, I was losing it over such a small amount of money. I don't know why it happened like that, but it did, and by this point I was shaking with rage. I called the children to double check that none of them had moved it that morning, which they hadn't so I called his mobile.

When he answered I said "you've taken thirteen pounds out of B's money box". He was silent for a second and told me he hadn't. I told him I knew he had because I had checked, and it wasn't the children, and he took a breath and said that it wasn't him, and that one of the children must have stolen it instead.

What happened next is a bit of a blur. I know that I shouted something down the phone and that it involved a lot of "fuck" variations, but aside from that, the details are sketchy. All of those terrible, gut wrenching words came flowing out and after I hung up, and as the children stood looking at me, I told them that I had had enough, and that it was all over. My hands were shaking so violently that I couldn't hold or do anything for at least ten minutes, and as had happened to me a couple of times before, it felt like two years of suppressed anger was surfacing all at the same time.

When he got home that night, he didn't speak to me at all. He did his usual routine of being aggressive and scary, but it didn't work on me this time. I hadn't cooked his dinner for the first time ever, despite making everyone else's, and he was visibly shocked and *very* angry. He sat in the armchair in front of the TV like nothing had happened, and I walked up behind him and said clearly and surely:

"I want a divorce. I've had enough."

I was shaking, and expected him to turn around but he didn't. He carried on watching the football, and said "ok" and that was that.

Reliving this time in my life is like talking about someone else. I can't even imagine allowing myself to be treated in this way now, and would fight absolutely anyone and anything to the death if they messed with my children. Back then though it was very different as you now know, and I can only refer to it in the terms that I have already used.

There is no doubt for me that this time was my most devastating Dark Night of The Soul, and had I not encountered it, I dread to think where I might be or what else I might have been pushed through next. I hit rock-bottom and then went a bit further down for good measure, and whilst I know it's difficult for those who love me to hear about how low I became, it's not difficult for me to talk about, and I think it's necessary.

I've done some stupid things in my lifetime. I've got drunk and stolen "For Sale" signs from the front gardens of houses. I've taken drugs and spent way too much time looking at the night sky as a result. I've had one-night stands with people I probably shouldn't have and who I've never seen again, but they're the kind of mistakes that were almost a rite of passage. I can't ever say that staying in this relationship was a mistake because I have a beautiful, funny and amazing daughter as a result of it, but *within* what happened, I *did* make mistakes, and big ones at that too.

I had to rebuild my life again, from scratch. At first, he wouldn't leave, and it was incredibly difficult as I was in his Dad's house, but about three months after I told him I wanted a divorce, he moved out and we were on our own again. It felt scary but incredible. The children were happier and I could start to help them process and deal with everything we had gone through. Money was of course, a huge issue and not only did I have nothing left, but my credit score was nothing short of diabolical. There had been hundreds of missed payments, unauthorised overdraft charges, and loans I hadn't known anything about, and it had left me right in the middle of a severe financial shit-storm. I *had* to move out of the house because it was too weird being there when it belonged to his family. We needed to feel free and safe, and I couldn't be sure that he wouldn't somehow manage to somehow get a key, so I started to look for somewhere else for us to live.

Finding somewhere we could afford and that would accept someone who was on benefits was a total nightmare. When I did find a house that was big enough and in the right place for the kids to carry on at school, I was told I would need to pay six months' rent in advance. There was *no way* I had access to that kind of money, and it felt like my life was about to be snatched away from me again.

I met my then best friend for lunch one morning the week I was told, and as I told her my predicament the tears readily fell from my eyes. It all felt hopeless and I just didn't know what I was going to do. We both sat in the restaurant together crying quietly, with tears running down our faces and our hands entwined; like best friends do. It was then that she offered to lend me the money to pay my rent. I was astonished and the tears that had started to wain suddenly renewed their vigour. We sat there together hugging, crying and talking for some time, and it was with her kindness and trust in me, that I was able to move into my new home a month later. We had the new beginning that I had been dreaming of, for what had seemed like forever.

It hasn't always been easy. But for the most part it's been pretty incredible, and along the way I've learnt so much about myself that I won't ever doubt myself again. That's another real gift. I've found a spiritual path that not only serves me, but is part of who I am and what I'm made from, and I have the most incredible relationships as a direct result of having to do such a huge amount of work on myself that I'm a completely different person now. Or was I just lost all along and have returned to myself? I'm still not sure I've quite figured that one out yet.

My Mum has a saying, and whenever I think about what happened, it comes into my head:

"Even a worm will turn."

It's true. Even when you think that there's no hope left, and even when everything seems stacked against you, there's always the possibility of a single moment that will transform it all. The times that I couldn't stand up for myself and the children within my second marriage really don't matter in the long run, because the only time that matters, is the one when I did. That *one time* the worm turned, negates all the times when it didn't. It might have been a rough journey, but the point of rotation was transformative in more ways than one, and overall, it's a series of mistakes that I'm more than happy to have made. And in the end, who wants to be perfect anyway?

P.S.

There are so many lessons that could be taken from this Not Normal Thing that happened in my life: boundaries, listening to your instincts, dropping your ego, learning how to support your own spiritual needs, helping an addict, self-confidence, overcoming fear, how to survive abuse... *so* many things. But when I thought about what it is I *really* want you to take away from it, and if there was only one thing that needed to be said, it was very clear that despite their validity, it was none of the above.

Once everything was out in the open and I had started to make strides to change my situation, I had lots of support from amazing people, and lots of advice - all of which helped. But there is one thing that no-one ever said to me that I wish they had:

"I see you, and I don't think any less of you."

Being in an abusive relationship, whether it's physical abuse, mental abuse, or both, brings up a ton of negative emotions and one of the biggest is shame. I felt ashamed that I had allowed myself to become "this". I felt embarrassed that I had accepted and believed the things I had been told, and I knew that once the people around me knew, they would probably think I was stupid. It was a thought I couldn't bear. Why not? Because when everything else in your life is destroyed, the only thing you have left is the people around you, the ones who aren't directly involved, but are part of your life. Considering the thought that they might think less of you leaves you with, well... nothing. I don't mean the people who judge you and walk away as a result; fuck them. You don't need that negativity in your life. I mean the ones who stick around, and still love you but that you know have at some point thought or said "wtf was she thinking?! Why didn't she just leave?!".

Of course, unless you've been through abuse yourself, you simply won't understand how anyone can allow themselves to be kept in that type of situation, but please take it from someone who knows, that it's not as simple as just leaving. If it was, there wouldn't be millions of people suffering in abusive relationships right now. It's complex, confusing and terrifyingly destructive. Leaving takes infinite amounts of strength and determination but also lays you bare to the unknown, which is also terrifying and can leave you feeling incredibly alone and somewhat bereft.

The truth of it all is, that we *all* make mistakes. There isn't a single person on the planet who's perfect. In fact, I like to say that we are all perfectly imperfect and I love the people in my life *because* of their flaws, not in spite of them. If we accept that we ourselves aren't perfect, then it's only right and fair that we allow others the same privilege.

It took me even more courage to tell people what I was (and had) been going through, than it did to actually leave. In fact, although leaving was incredibly difficult and scary, it felt relatively easy by comparison. I didn't want my friends and family to see me as stupid and pathetic, which is how I felt. I'm an intelligent woman and somehow, I had become someone else who didn't even have a semblance of that anymore. I didn't want them to look at me and say the things we know have been said over and over about people who stay in abusive relationships, and I felt like they would lose respect for me. I was scared that nothing would ever be the same and I would lose the only thing I had left.

My usual P.S. normally guides you to look at your own life and shows you how to apply a new way of thinking or being, and of course that can also be applied to anyone who is reading this and (fortunately) hasn't ever gone through any type of abuse. If that's you, I'm glad you haven't found yourself in that position, truly, and I ask you to try and understand how it *might* feel, so that if you ever know someone who is, you feel able to say to them "I see you, and I don't think any less of you".

And for those of you who have been there, or are there now, or in fact for anyone who has ever felt overwhelming shame for any mistake they have ever made, I want you to know that truly and deeply, and from the bottom of my heart and soul;

I see you. And I most definitely don't think any less of you. You are miraculous, and most beautifully, perfectly imperfect.

P.P.S

Empath = a person with the paranormal ability to perceive the mental or emotional state of another individual.

They are highly attuned to other people's moods, good and bad. They feel everything, sometimes to an extreme. They take on negativity such as anger or anxiety, which can be exhausting for them.

There are clear signs as to whether you may be an Empath or not. If you are someone who

- has major empathy for others
- feels easily overwhelmed

- has strong intuition (not to be confused with actually listening to it - having it and listening to it are two very different things!)
- loves nature
- dislikes crowds
- cares deeply for people
- is good at solving problems
- is highly sensitive
- suffers with anxiety
- has little control over your emotions
- has a history of trying to fix people

then it's highly likely that you're an Empath.

It can be really difficult to keep yourself grounded and on an even keel if you haven't learnt how to protect yourself from absorbing the emotions and energies of those around you. As well as that, it's also really difficult to work out how you feel when the feelings you are experiencing aren't your own, especially if you don't even realise that that's what's happening.

There are also those people who have a gift of seeking out Empaths, especially ones who haven't honed their skill yet, as a way of creating the kind of life they want for themselves. If you do a quick internet search, you'll find loads of information about the Empath and Narcissist relationship, which again is not uncommon, and is incredibly destructive.

You might have heard the well-known saying repeated by a lot of Empaths:

"Being an Empath is both a blessing and a curse"

I don't agree at all and I would ask you to consider what seeing yourself in this way might subconsciously lead you to feel or show up to be. When the right steps and actions are taken, being an Empath is always a blessing. Being able to tell how people are feeling without them saying, is an incredible gift, and sometimes it can be a saving grace.

In my experience there are lots of ways to protect your energy and ensure that you keep yourself safe which I'll share below, but don't forget to research your own and try anything that feels good to you. There is no "one size fits all" as far as getting clear about which emotions are yours and which aren't, because we are all different, but if you follow some simple guidelines, you'll most certainly find something that works in the way you need it to.

Salt

Hippocrates was said to have discovered the healing properties of salt after witnessing how it healed fishermen's hands. Salt is purifying and healing, and is great for clearing away negative energies. I use it a lot in Witchcraft. Add Himalayan Pink salt in a body scrub, or just add it to your bath and it will do the rest of the work. Please check with your doctor first if you have any underlying health conditions that might be affected by this.

Crystals

There are so many different crystals available to us, and carrying them on your person or putting them under your pillow is a really good way of transmuting and shifting energy. There are definitely specific crystals that are said to be particularly helpful to Empaths such as Haematite, but in my experience, it's better to go with one that really speaks to you. You'll know which one that is when you're stood in front of the crystal shelf in the shop! Trust your instincts and allow your higher self to choose the right one for you. My personal favourites are always Rose Quartz and Obsidian, and as I have already said, if you don't feel able to pick your own, Haematite is a good place to start. Shove them in your bra or pocket, and put them under your pillow at night to help clear any negative energy that you may have picked up but don't forget to cleanse and charge them first.

To cleanse a crystal, I prefer to either wash it in mineral water or a natural spring (there are some crystals that you shouldn't get wet so check first and use the smoke cleansing method for those. Haematite happens to fall into that category), or smoke cleanse with Sage (don't be tempted to use Palo Santo or anything else for this, as it doesn't do quite the same thing).

To charge it, leave it on the window sill in either the sunshine or the moonlight (again, do whichever feels right for you as the Sun and the Moon have very different energy).

Movement

I generally like to avoid exercise, but without doubt, one of the easiest and quickest ways of shifting negative energy for me is movement. Go for a walk in nature, get out in the fresh air, or put some music on at home and shake it out! I do both, and it's inarguable that having a really good dance around your kitchen certainly makes you feel brighter, lighter and shifts your energy completely.

Grounding

Practice grounding yourself. If you are connected to the earth, and properly grounded, you are way more likely to repel other people's energy and feel better all round. It's easy to do and as long as you take the time to practice, soon enough you'll be able to do it in seconds if you need to. The great thing about it is that you can do it as often as you need, and anywhere! So, if you're at a party and feeling a bit wobbly, you can take a minute to ground yourself and you should instantly feel some relief.

Make sure your feet connected to the floor, flat on the ground with bare feet is best, and imagine big, strong roots coming out from the soles of them and send them down into the earth below. Imagine them going right down into the centre of the earth, right at the core, and see them in your mind's eye as they become one with the soil. Spend some time taking some deep calming breaths, and really visualise it. It can look however you want it to, that part is up to you. It's as easy as that. Repeat throughout your day as necessary.

Sound/Music/Singing

The vibration of sound is a wonderful clearing energy. It's a scientific fact that some frequencies of sound have specific healing effects, so it should be no surprise that using sound to shift stuck energy works. Use whatever you like; Binaural beats off YouTube, a beautiful choral recording, a bit of Beethoven, or the latest hit by Taylor Swift… it doesn't matter! Just crank it up and really give yourself to it. Immerse yourself into the sound and if you happen to sing along too, all the better!

Shielding

Shielding is a way of forming a protective barrier around your aura. It's similar to the grounding technique I use and the same principles apply. Practice will mean that you can use it where you like and as many times as you need, but at first make sure you take the time to ensure you're happy with how it feels.

Make sure you're comfortable, relax and close your eyes. Imagine that you are floating somewhere beautiful. It can be in another dimension, or above a beautiful woodland, the details are up to you. See yourself floating in your chosen location, and imagine that there is some form of chain or barrier all around you. It could be a chain of flowers, or a bubble, again it doesn't matter - choose whatever you want to, and once you can see that barrier all around your body, surrounding you from head to toe with no breaks, imagine it being filled with an astonishing light. It can be any colour, but it has to completely fill the space around you within the bubble you have formed. Nothing negative can get past the shield, only good. You are now shielded.

Above all, be discerning. If being around someone doesn't feel right, remove yourself from them when you can, and do one of the techniques above, or one that you find yourself, and don't feel bad about it. It doesn't necessarily mean that person isn't nice, it simply means that your energies don't mix well, so treat everyone with love but don't be afraid to move away from people if you need to.

I hope this gives you a very basic insight into a topic that has overwhelming amounts of information available on it, and goes some way to helping you understand yourself a little more. If you identify with being an Empath, don't shy away from it as you can't change it, just make this amazing superpower work for you instead!

Not Normal Things #7
"Dolly Daydream"

I was a really cute looking little girl, and although it might seem strange for me to say that about myself, it's true. I had white blonde hair and bright blue eyes, with chubby little thighs and appley cheeks. My Mum has always said that I was an angel who was really easy to look after because I was quite happy playing by myself in my own little world. It's true, I was. As I got older, I loved being by myself just doing the things that I enjoyed, and even as an adult, I still do.

I was born in March and my Sun sign is Pisces. I know that not everyone is convinced by astrology and its ascribed meanings, but I am, and if you read a comprehensive description of what it means to be Pisces, then you're pretty much reading an entirely accurate description of my personality.

As such, I'm fully aware of all the things I'm really good at, and all the things I'm not. I tend to be a dreamer, imagining a utopian world in which magickal things happen every minute of the day. I am ridiculously optimistic about how things will turn out, unless of course something interrupts that trajectory, in which case I can quickly become wholeheartedly disheartened and incredibly sad. I'm a hopeless romantic, and would sacrifice anything to ensure that the people around me know just how much I love them at any given time. My personality is floaty and ethereal, over-exaggerated and spontaneous, and without some kind of anchor, I'd almost certainly spend my days willingly staring into the magickal and beautiful universe that I'm very capable of creating in my mind. To those that don't know me well I appear to be an extrovert who is very self-assured but I'm actually incredibly shy and introverted, with a sometimes-crushing lack of confidence. I love looking out of windows, and could spend hours and hours doing just that with no agenda or perceived outcome at all.

I'm also incredibly stubborn, fiercely independent and wildly impatient. I don't like being told what to do by anyone even if I know it's in my best interests. In fact, other than my Mum, there has only ever been one other person who has managed to tame that particular trait without argument, which believe me is quite an achievement, but who's success in that, is rooted in the point I made above about me happily doing anything for the people I truly love, including challenging my own shortcomings.

Growing up, there was a phrase I heard a lot. The phrase itself is not unusual, but the frequency that it was used in relation to me, was. I heard it from Aunties and Uncles, my Nanny and Grandad, and not just in direct conversation but in overheard ones that they had too.

"She's in a dolly daydream again", they'd say.

Lots of people fall into a Dolly Daydream, especially children. It's that thing where someone seems to go into a trance for a minute and their eyes glaze over (just in case you don't happen to know what I'm talking about), and it's always been something that I've done a lot.

Sometimes people would wave their hands in front of my face to snap me out of it, and as I was abruptly brought back to reality, I'd hear my Mum telling them not to do that.

"You shouldn't do that" she'd say. "She obviously needs it. If you see someone having a daydream, just leave them alone."

I always loved that she did that. I mean, it's not like it's a planned thing, and I agree with her. If someone has zoned out for a minute, they obviously have something that they need to process in a different way to usual. Maybe.

It's not difficult to see, given my nature, how people often seemed to think I was often off in a world of my own, and that's no big shakes, but three years ago something happened that altered the way I saw these childhood realities and it's not only interesting, but has been incredibly insightful for me.

I love driving, and I'm a good driver too. I passed my test first time when I was seventeen, and being able to get to everywhere I need to go easily (especially with four children) has always been a godsend.

In 2017 my eldest daughter and I (she was sixteen at the time), were in the car driving to somewhere of no significance. We were talking about something-and-nothing, and generally passing the time to wherever it was we were going. During our journey on familiar and well-travelled local roads, at some point near the middle of the trip, and on a straight stretch of road, I hit the kerb quite badly and had no idea how I'd done it. We were both surprised, and my daughter asked me what had happened. I didn't know, and I told her as much, putting it down to one of those little freak momentary happenings that you can't really explain. I thought about it on and off for the rest of the journey because it wasn't just a little bump and genuinely didn't make sense, but eventually got distracted by the events of the rest of the day and thought nothing more of it.

Two days later we were both in the car together again on a quick run to the supermarket, and using the same roads as usual. This time it was on the way back that the very same thing happened, and as the car hit the kerb and jolted us both in our seats, my daughter exclaimed:

"What the hell… why do you keep doing that?"

As with the time before, I didn't know the answer, and all I could offer was that maybe I was a bit tired or something, but I was genuinely confused and couldn't find any real kind of plausible explanation.

I guess hindsight would tell you that you probably shouldn't be in a car if you're having weird little experiences that affect your driving skills, but they were two isolated incidents of no great significance (or so I thought) and I told myself that maybe I'd just not been concentrating as much as I should have been; I'd pay more attention from now on and it would be fine.

Five days passed and everything was fine. It was mid-afternoon, school turning out time actually, and I'd been to the shops with my youngest daughter who was six. She was in her car seat in the back behind me, and we were about five minutes (if that) from home. It was a nice day, sunny and dry, and the radio was playing. I was watching the road ahead of me and listening to my daughter sing. And then, in the blink of an eye, there was nothing.

There was no darkness, and no light. There was no sound, and no silence. There wasn't a realisation that there was "nothing", or any sense of panic or fear either…there was simply nothing. No time, no space, no anything. It was as if someone had flicked a switch and I didn't exist anymore; nothing existed, not even the possibility of existence. I saw nothing, heard nothing and felt nothing without realising that there was even nothing.

The bump (and the sound of it) was the first thing moment of awareness I had again, and a milli-second later I heard my six-year-old ask me what was happening. I saw the house in front of us grow closer as the car travelled over the path, and into its front garden. I honestly don't know how I managed to steer the car in that short space of time, or stop it from hitting anything or anyone, but I did, and suddenly we were back on the road. I slammed on my brakes and sat in the driver's seat in total shock, shaking uncontrollably.

The little voice of my daughter came from behind me and asked me if I was ok. I wasn't. I was scared and confused and had *no idea* what had happened, but I told her I was fine. After having sat still for a while, I very slowly drove the couple of minutes back home, parked the car, took my daughter inside and hung up my car keys. I picked up the phone and called the doctors surgery to make an emergency appointment and by some miracle, had called just after a last-minute cancelation, so could be seen ten minutes later.

I left my eldest son in charge of his little sister and walked the short distance to the doctors, all the while replaying what had just happened in my head. I went over it again and again, and no matter how hard I tried I couldn't understand what had happened.

The doctor asked me why I was there, as they always do, and through tears and shock I relayed the story of what had played out less than half an hour before. It was hard to explain to her because I had nothing *to* explain other than that one minute, I was fine, and the next, there was nothing. She told me that she thought I had had a seizure, and although I should try not to worry, she was sending me straight to hospital.

The next twenty-four hours passed in somewhat of a blur. I was no longer allowed to drive (not that I wanted to anyway - I was *way* too scared for that) and was sent to hospital for an emergency MRI scan. One of my friends took me and stayed with me until the early hours of the morning when I was released and told that they couldn't do it that night, and to come back in the morning. I went back home and in between bouts of tears and fear, I slept.

In the weeks that followed I had numerous scans and tests, and a lot more seizures. Some were big and some were small. Some in the day and some during the night when I was asleep. Sometimes I would get pulled into that vacuous place where there was nothing, and sometimes I would stutter, stammer, fall over or lose the ability to speak the words that I had always so easily been able to speak. My short-term memory became much worse and I became easily confused. I was more tired than I'd ever been before, and I was frightened too.

Four months later I was diagnosed with Epilepsy; temporal lobe focal absent seizures to be precise, and with that diagnosis came a whole host of information that was insanely scary and incredibly interesting. I also had my driving licence revoked and was told that I was no longer allowed to be on my own anywhere. I could no longer lock a bathroom door, ride a horse or get on a bike, and had to stop doing many of the things that I had made part of my life, either because I wasn't allowed to do them anymore, or I felt too ill to do them anyway. My whole life was turned on its head, and I didn't know what to do, or how to feel, about any of it.

187

To other people, when I have an absent seizure, I don't look much different. I don't shake or convulse as people do with other types of seizures; I just look like I've gone into a daydream. My children say that I look vacant, but not scary. They say they can now tell but they're not really sure how. Early on they couldn't distinguish between a mild trance like state and a full-blown seizure, but they soon became familiar with how I presented during a more serious episode, and would tell me how it looked to them after I came out of it. It's interesting that I usually simply stop what I'm doing and appear to just be in a deep, deep daydream.

My neurologist who is the sweetest, kindest consultant I've ever come across, told me that it's unusual for people to develop this type of seizure in adulthood as it's normally most common in children, and the likelihood is that I've had it all my life and because it wasn't as severe as it is now, it's been mistaken for me being (in his words) "away with the fairies". It seems that it's entirely possible that for at least *some* of the times that those around me thought I was just a bit of a dreamer as a little girl, I was in fact having absent seizures.

Of course, that's not to say this was the case all of the time. There will obviously be plenty of occasions when I was simply just having fun with my own thoughts, just like most people do, but it is crazy to think that some of the things that I (and other people too) have put down to my nature, have in fact been as a result of epilepsy instead. Not that it would have made any difference, and it didn't negatively affect me in any way really, but it does go to show that things are not always what they seem. Even for me, the version of myself that I had been quite happy to be up to that point, was about to undergo a huge overhaul; a "level-up", and one that would once again make me face some of the shadow parts of myself that I'd previously, blissfully ignored.

Being forced to relinquish all the things that have given you your independence and enabled you to survive without any help at all, would be a struggle for anyone. But for me, with my unforgiving and relentless independent streak, it almost broke me.

I could no longer hop in the car and nip to the supermarket or take the children where they needed to go. Nothing happened quickly anymore and I was forced to rely on inconsistent and unreliable public transport. I couldn't visit the people I wanted to visit, or get to the many hospital appointments I needed to get to with ease. Worst of all, I couldn't do the "fluffy" things that people like to do. I couldn't just pop to TK Maxx and spend an hour looking at cushions, candles and kitchenware. I couldn't go to the spiritual emporiums that had previously provided me with stocks of incense and crystals. Going to the cinema became a total mission, and much more expensive. Getting to the yard to see the horses was almost impossible and became more of a stressful event than something I loved. It sounds unimportant, but these are the fluffy things that aren't a necessity, but make life fun and keep us motivated. More importantly, they're also the kind of things that keep your mental health in check. I'm not naïve or deluded enough to realise that I'm incredibly privileged to be able to have enjoyed these things in my life in the first place, and neither am I ignorant enough to think that many people simply don't have access to these sorts of luxuries, but that doesn't render them irrelevant.

People with Epilepsy are much more likely to suffer with severe depression and although I didn't understand why in the beginning, it very quickly became clear. Aside from feeling really ill most of the time, and having to process all the new information about yourself and how your body works, you also have to accept that your life has completely changed in every way possible. Not being able to carry out everyday tasks in the same way is frustrating, and as I've already said, not being able to do all the fun stuff that you usually do, is incredibly hard. I felt unable to be a good mother. I couldn't cook every night, or clean the house as well as I would usually. I got behind with lots of things, and didn't feel like I would ever catch up again. I missed seeing the people I usually easily spent time with, and doing the things I loved doing freely, and amongst feeling all of these things, I couldn't ask for help.

A lot of people offered help but I just didn't want it. People I wasn't even that close to would message and offer to take me shopping, or to hospital appointments. My family and close friends would offer to help with anything I needed, and in the beginning, I would thank them but add that I was ok and didn't need anything. For me, admitting that I was struggling was like saying that I was vulnerable and weak, and that was something I simply didn't want to do.

Despite the protestations of my Neurologist, I decided that going on medication was something I really didn't want to do either, so I didn't in the beginning. I did a ton of research into the best holistic treatments for Epilepsy and started doing those. I was lucky enough to be good friends with a very talented man who helped me work out the best supplements to take and when to take them, so I did that too. I stopped drinking and eating anything processed, especially anything with artificial sweetener in. I worked really hard at getting my regime sorted out so that I always got enough sleep, and could rest when I needed to. I also immersed myself into intense spiritual practices including Shamanic journeying and past-life regression. I made some progress, and the bigger seizures stopped. I became more used to public transport schedules which made life a little simpler as I could set some kind of routine, but none of it was easy.

I had a couple of great friends who would fetch me if we were going somewhere, or take me shopping or to hospital appointments, and I was (and still am) very grateful to them for those things, but I still really missed the fluffy stuff and being able to do things for my children that I had previously taken for granted (like taking them to college). I was trying desperately hard to manage everything, but the truth was, I felt completely and utterly lost.

My primary seizures had completely stopped, but increasingly I felt unwell often, and the mini seizures were happening on a daily basis and seemed to be getting worse. I spent a lot of time at home and despite having people around me that I loved, and who loved me, I felt incredibly lonely. Suddenly having so much taken away from me meant I felt isolated, and I knew that I had to make some changes, and probably ones I didn't want to make.

I had a lot of time to think, and the many hours of soul searching that I did, I discovered that the level at which I was independent, was not always a good thing. Sure, it meant I'd been able to raise my children on my own, and do all of the things that some people would ask for help to do, but it also meant that, in this case, I was suffering. I asked myself why I couldn't say yes to someone offering help, and it became clear that I definitely saw it as some sort of failure on my part and more so that I didn't want to be a burden to anyone. But struggling the way I was just wasn't ok, and certainly wasn't necessary, so I decided to work at allowing more for myself.

It sounds easy, but believe me it wasn't! As well as asking for help, I also discovered that my propensity to be a "yes" person was still lurking in the background despite me having done personal work on that some time before, so that had to go too.

I started saying no to people who wanted my time when I didn't feel well enough to give it. Then I started saying no to things that I just really didn't want to do, and it was life changing. I felt empowered and genuinely like I was really caring for myself. I wasn't mean about it, but I was clear and completely sure of myself, and whilst some people were surprised at first, it didn't take long before the new boundaries I had set were respected and life got a lot easier.

Asking for help, or saying yes to it when it was offered, was more difficult. I felt guilty for taking up people's time and would ask them over and over if they were sure it was ok. I felt like I was failing a lot of the time, because I couldn't do these things for myself, but I started putting my ego in check and just getting on with it, and before very long it became somewhat bearable.

Over time and with practice, asking for help actually became completely normal - my new normal - and I found that it also made me more able to give too. I hadn't realised before, but by accepting or asking for help when I needed it, I had more capacity, time and motivation to do things for other people, and not because I had to, but because I wanted to. Life once again started to feel much less challenging and I found myself feeling much more positive about this whole new way of showing up in the world.

Having said that, I had developed a facial tick that meant my nose scrunched up repeatedly (I call it my rabbit face and it still happens now on days when Epilepsy grabs me a bit tighter) and I sometimes became unable to speak the sentences that were perfectly formed in my head. They just wouldn't come out of my mouth when I tried to say them, and it was becoming more and more frustrating. Although conventional medication would never be my first or preferred choice of treatment (at least not without trying other remedies beforehand) I couldn't see another way of reducing the mini seizures I was experiencing all day every day, and my mental health was becoming affected by them too, so I called the relevant people and got a prescription for the Epilepsy medication that my consultant had wanted me to take since the day he had diagnosed me.

Going on Keppra was a really big deal for me. I started on a low dose which would be increased gradually. This was so that I would get used to the many side effects that were almost guaranteed, and also so that my mini seizures could be monitored and I wouldn't be taking a larger dosage than necessary.

It was ok to start with, I was a bit tired and had bouts of severe nausea, but nothing too serious. In terms of my seizures though, nothing changed so after a couple of weeks my dose was increased.

The nausea didn't ease, nor did the tiredness, and they were joined by a lot of other side effects too. Insomnia joined the party for a week or two, as did an increase in my migraines (something I had been diagnosed with since the age of fifteen) but I carried on and they eased off after a while. My seizures didn't though, so once again my dosage was increased.

This went on until I was on one dose increase away from the maximum allowed, and the side effects got much worse as the dosage increased. It was a really difficult time but with the help of my children (who were seventeen, sixteen, fifteen and six) I got through it until one day, my seizures stopped altogether.

Returning to feeling "normal" again was incredible. No more facial twitch, no more vacant stares not knowing what the fuck was going on once I came round again, and no more having to wait for my brain to catch up to finish a sentence. The side effects had completely gone and I finally felt like I could start to get my life back on track. I started riding again, I went back to the gym to lose some of the weight I'd gained in the months previously, and life felt really good for the first time in a while.

Things were good for a year, and I was doing well, until the long-term side effects of the medication I was taking started taking hold, and then very quickly, things changed once again.

When my consultant put me on Keppra, he told me very clearly that the most serious side effect was that it can cause severe depression, and suicidal tendencies. It wasn't ever hidden from me, in fact quite the opposite, and it was the one thing I was terrified of.

It crept up quickly but quietly. I've been suicidal three times in my life and it's not something I talk about lightly, but this last time was different. I didn't encounter the dark thoughts I'd had previously, entering my head and pushing their way in at unexpected times, and I didn't feel like I was drowning in a sea of treacle like I had before. It sounds trite, but I just didn't want to live any more. Don't get me wrong, I felt low, and I would cry a lot, but it *felt* different.

Like when I was reading something or watching TV, I would suddenly just think "I don't want to be alive anymore" (read that in the sort of voice you hear on an infomercial and that's what it felt like; not dark or menacing, just factual, and weirdly, rather jolly).

I could also observe those thoughts and feelings when they came, and I *knew* that they weren't actually mine, even though they felt very real; it's hard to explain. I'm not saying that I wasn't very depressed because I definitely was, but it felt like someone or something else, was forcing me to feel and think that way, and I knew it was the meds.

I allowed it to go on for about six months because I didn't want the seizures back, but then it became something I really couldn't fight anymore, so I called the hospital to try and speak to my consultant. I got through to his secretary who told me I could have an appointment in six weeks' time at which point I broke down and told her I probably wouldn't be around by then. She asked me what was wrong and I told her I was suicidal and didn't know what to do. I had stopped doing any of the things I usually did, and every day felt like I was swimming against an incredibly fierce and constant tide. My consultant called half an hour later, we talked for a while, and told me he would speak to me the next day to arrange an appointment.

The next morning my phone rang and true to his word, it was my consultant. He asked me how I was and I told him through gasped breaths and an influx of emotion that I couldn't hold back, that I just felt like I couldn't carry on anymore. He arranged for me to see him the next day, and as I sat in front of him and broke down again, he took my hand and told me that everything would be alright, and that there was no doubt that the Keppra was making me feel the way I did.

It was a complex process, but the positive effects of coming off the medication happened quickly. After a week I felt less depressed than I had been, even though there was still a long way to go, and I could see the light at the end of what had been a very dark tunnel. It was suggested to me that I try different meds, but I decided that I would stop taking any medication at all, and see what happened.

After a few months, I was totally free from any kind medication and felt like myself once again. It was amazing to feel so mentally well, and although there had been some side effects from the withdrawal (like weight gain, fatigue and dizziness) I was happy to have made it out the other side.

As I write this, it's been about eight months since then, and navigating my Epilepsy is still something that takes a lot of work and sometimes takes its toll on my mental health too. But what I've discovered is that although I have to take it into consideration, I certainly don't need to let it control my life.

It took a while to adjust to, but I'm back at the gym trying to lose the weight I put on, and I got my licence back a while ago too. I suffer quite badly with mini seizures; they happen more than several times every day, but that's things like losing words, getting words mixed up, forgetting things that I really shouldn't be forgetting, and generally seeming like a bit of a dim-whit at times, so I'm managing that the best I can and am looking at other options to get those things under control.

Epilepsy has taught me so much about myself, and it's also taught me a lot about other people too.

I've learnt that I can be independent without sacrifices to my own wellbeing and life. That asking for help not only means I don't struggle in silence, but that it gives those who care for me the chance to show that care in real terms.

I've learnt that sometimes, when you think you've nailed something like boundary setting, all you've really done is made a slight improvement, and that there are always more advancements you can make. There's no finish line when it comes to personal development.

I've learnt that people love helping, and they all like it for different reasons. Some like it because it makes them feel good about themselves, some like it because it means other people think well of them, and some like it because they know you are happy, safe and well. In the long run, their reason for helping is none of my business, and if it feels right, then there's no reason not to graciously accept.

I've learnt that how I use my diagnosis is up to me, and that whilst I accept that things have definitely changed for me, that doesn't mean I have to let it define me. I can do anything I put my mind to, I just might have to do it in a different way to everyone else, which is definitely not a new theme for me!

To a certain extent, I have had to redefine who I am as a result of a lifelong condition that cannot be cured. But that's ok because what it's meant is that I have had to take a long, hard look at myself, and make some very necessary changes to who I am, and the way I show up for myself in the world.

In the end, it begs the question… am I really a Dolly Daydream?

Yes. I'm a Pisces so of course I am, by nature, and it seems, by genetic design as well.

P.S.

Having any kind of condition or illness is challenging and I certainly don't profess to have all the answers, or a magick wand. Actually, I do have one of those, but it won't help with this. I mean, if I did, I'd be sitting on one hell of a money pile right now! I do however, believe that we can help ease the process by learning new lessons about ourselves, and life in general, when we are faced with such a crisis.

For me, it's Epilepsy, but for you it could be anything; Diabetes, Cancer, MS, Fibromyalgia, Migraine, Hypermobility, COPS or any one of the thousands of illnesses and conditions that collectively, we suffer from. Of course, they're all different, and some more life threatening than others, but this is not about comparison, it's about how you cope with whatever you're going through and what *you* can do to make it easier.

At first, it seems like a really Not Normal Thing to be diagnosed with something that changes your life, but in reality, there are so many of us who are going through exactly the same, I'd say that sadly, it's probably more normal than most things. But I know from experience that it *really* doesn't feel that way in the beginning. It's a shock, and takes some getting used to. You have all this new information that you have to process, and everything feels up in the air and you have no idea where it's all going to land, or if indeed it ever will.

All of that is ok. It's absolutely ok to feel lost and all-at-sea to start with, in fact I think it's not only natural, but necessary. It's vital to feel everything deeply so that you can start to make some kind of sense of it all, but I think that there comes a point where you have to decide how this is going to work for you, and to what extent you're going to change your life as a result. Please don't mistake that sentiment for me saying that you must always have a positive attitude, or that any measure of the anguish or pain you feel is your fault if you don't; there's a lot of spiritual gangsters who will tell you that your mindset causes your situations, and therefore illness is something you've brought upon yourself, and whilst there are elements of that I agree with, I think it's widely used as a tool to guilt people into pretending to be "better people" and that is certainly *not* what I am trying to do.

What I *am* saying, is that no matter what it is that is happening to you, you must remember the things that *are in your control* and do everything you can (even the difficult stuff) to make sure that they are working in the best way for you.

None of us stay the same throughout our lives, it's not possible. Even if it's only by circumstance and not by choice, we all evolve as we travel through the journey that we set out upon. If you are in the same position as me, in that you have (or are going through) some kind of health experience, I want you to understand that within that, you don't have to evolve on "it's" terms, but that you can most definitely evolve on yours.

What is it that you're facing?

What is it that scares you most about it, and why does that scare you so much?

What is it that most upsets you in this situation? And why does it trigger that upset?

What emotional wounds can you heal? Are you acknowledging them and changing your behaviour accordingly going forwards?

Most importantly, *what can you do* to ease any of those things?

The one thing everyone who is facing illness of any kind has, is time to themselves. Often you are forced to rest, whether you like it or not, and whilst it can be hard to spend time with your thoughts in particularly challenging times, it's also a great time to really look as some of the questions above, and work out solutions to the answers you get.

In situations like this, having to redefine yourself isn't always something we choose to do, but it's definitely easier if you choose to take control of it and make changes that not only benefit your own growth, but your wellbeing and lifestyle too.

I know it's scary, and I know it feels shit sometimes, but flailing around in the darkness not having any kind of plan is even worse, and the only way you can combat that is to really get to know yourself and change the bits of you that need changing in order to move forwards.

For me, that was dropping my ego and allowing people to help me, as well as setting stronger boundaries for myself around what it was I said yes to. For you it might be totally different things, and there are a million variations on the possibilities, but digging deep and unpicking the feelings that you have, is the only way to determine what needs working on. Doing so can only bring about beneficial change.

I'm grateful to Epilepsy for showing me parts of myself that needed healing. I wouldn't have seen them had I not been forced to in this way, and doing the inner work to rectify those things can never be a bad thing. I hope that whatever it is you are facing, and no matter how serious or life-changing it is, this helps you to see some of the positives within it for you, and enables you to redefine yourself in a way that *you* choose.

ʿNot Normal Things #8
Loved, Lost and a Timely Tomcatʾ
Part 1

I can't remember a significantly long period of time in my life in which I didn't have animals. Growing up we always had dogs, normally two at that, and often a sprinkling of other things too. There were the two budgerigars that my Dad brought home one day out of the blue, the tortoise that turned up in the same way, and the odd goldfish from the annual fairground win.

Just like many people, I really love animals. They not only fill me with great joy, but have also been part of the work I do as there is a language that they speak that can be heard, if you listen in the right way. It's not just domestic animals either. Last year on our holiday in The Highlands, my partner and I saw wild animals including a red squirrel, a golden eagle, deer and highland cows, and it's hard to put into words how much happiness it brought me.

Over the last twenty-three years, I've had the pleasure of owning eight dogs, three guinea pigs, two rabbits, six cats and a horse. That in itself is nothing out of the ordinary, but out of all of those, only three of the dogs lived past the age of five, and they are the three that went to live with other people after my first divorce (through circumstance, not by any choice of mine). Not a single one of the other dogs survived for longer than five years, the rabbits and guinea pigs only lived for two years or less, and only eighteen months after I got him, my horse died at the age of fourteen. I have two cats who seem to have passed this milestone point, just, and two who are under it. The other two died last year at the ages of five and two.

It's a very normal thing to lose an animal, awful, but normal nonetheless. But some of the animals I've had, have left as a result of unusual events, and most of them before the age of five, and that's why it is such a Not Normal Thing for me. Conversely, some of the animals I've had, *arrived* in an unusual way too, and whilst they may not have died, they have left my life in nearly as an unorthodox way as they entered.

Now I realise at this point that you might be raising serious questions about my capacity to care for animals, and trust me when I tell you that I've done that myself too, but please be reassured that I have loved and cared for each and every one of them, and have never done anything that might cause them any harm at all. I have struggled with the outcome of each of the situations more than anyone knows, and it's something that I've spent many, many hours thinking about and meditating on in a search for some sort of explanation or reason for it being the way it is, and has been. Could I have done things differently? Did I make the right choices? Why is it that it always happens to me? I drove myself mad with questions like these for a really long time and it's been a long and challenging road, and also one that I'm sure I'm not even at the end of quite yet. I've questioned my ability to care for the animals I've had, and replayed the actions I've taken once a problem was obvious, many times. But despite being my own worst critic, and usually finding it easy to blame myself for most things, I *do* know that not only am I a great animal guardian, but none of these things were my doing, or my fault. I also understand that they have all happened, as with everything in life, for a reason.

Pongo

Not long after we moved in together, my first husband and I got a dog. My sister and her boyfriend had rescued a dog that was going to be put to sleep, and a few weeks after they did, she had a litter of eight puppies. We had one of her puppies and we called him Pongo.

Pongo was a big dog. He was light chocolate brown with caramel eyebrows, white socks and had a light brown nose. He was the most incredible dog and I loved him more than I can accurately put into words. He was goofy and funny, and lolloped around like a baby elephant most of the time, but when he ran, he was *so* fast! He could take off from standing still and be at full pace in three strides, and if he saw a cat while he was off the lead, well, thank fuck that never happened outside of the garden!

He was four years old and perfectly healthy when we moved to a new house (you know, the one that we spent a load of money on and had to move due to police helicopters and dirty needles… that one). It was a great move for him because the garden was 150ft long and he absolutely loved it. He would spend most of the day wandering in and out freely, digging up anything that smelt remotely interesting, and burying anything that he wanted to hide.

One night in the summer of his fourth year, we had a dinner party for my Mum and Stepdad. They came over and we ate a lovely meal that I'd prepared, and drank lots of wine. It was really warm and I had left the back door open so that Pongo could go in and out as he pleased. At around midnight, he suddenly shot up from the dining room floor, scrambling on the wooden floor like Scooby Doo to get out as quickly as he could, and went tearing into the garden barking. I got up to go and call him as it was so late and the neighbours would definitely not have been amused at the volume of noise he was making, and just as I got to the back-door I heard him squeal.

It wasn't a noise I'd ever heard before, and I knew something was very, very wrong. I called him in a panic whilst opening the door wider so I could go out and find him, but as I did so, I saw him fall on the path outside in front of me and then, I saw all the blood.

I screamed and ran to him, still not knowing what the hell had happened. His intestines were spilling out of a massive hole that ran straight through his middle. It happened in seconds. My then husband ran down the garden to see if he could find anything to explain what had happened while I packed Pongo's stomach back into the hole in his side, and stuffed it with tea towels to stop the bleeding. We had all been drinking so my Mum called a taxi while I called the emergency vet and soon, we were on our way.

When we arrived, Pongo was conscious but obviously in a very bad way. They took him in and told us to wait. After half an hour the vet came to see us in the waiting room and told us that whatever had punctured him had gone straight through him and out the other side but miraculously had missed every major organ, so they were going to do what they could but it would be a case of waiting to see how his body reacted. We went home in total shock, and waited for a call.

It turned out that whilst gardening that week, the wheelbarrow was left in the middle of the very long garden, and on that awful night, Pongo had heard something (most likely a cat) and had took off at full throttle. In his bid to catch it, he had tried to jump the wheelbarrow and miscalculated, and as a result, he impaled himself on one of its handles - it went straight through the middle of him and out the other side. In the incredibly brave action of freeing himself so quickly from it, he had increased the size of the puncture wound significantly.

It was devastating, but when the vet called the next morning, he was positive, and asked us to go in. I was desperate to see him, and was told that he was very weak, very fragile but hadn't so far shown any signs of toxic shock (which was the biggest threat to his life). They said I could see him, but that he wasn't to get too excited and for us to remain calm. I went in alone, and when I got down on the floor to give him a love, he laid on my knee wagging his tail. I knew he was desperate to come home; it was written all over his face, and I asked the vet if it was possible. He said no, obviously, so I begged him. I told him that if Pongo stayed in the veterinary surgery, he would die, and that I knew he would be better off at home with me. He said that if there was no sign of infection by the next morning, he'd consider it, and that Pongo needed to rest, so I gave him a kiss on his big brown nose, and told him to be good. By the time we had made the five-minute car journey home, we had the call to tell us that Pongo had died. He was only four years old.

At the point at which this terrible event happened, I was still kind of half-in, half-out of the spiritual closet so to speak, and whilst I openly went through the very human and logical aspects of the grief that surrounds the loss of a beloved animal, I still needed a more esoteric explanation for it too.

I only explored those explanations in a basic way; one that reflected the small amount of time I gave to including more spiritual matters into my life at that point. As such, I could only find one answer to the complex question of why it had to be the way it was, but it gave me some comfort, and helped me make more sense out of a situation that seemed to have no sense in it at all.

I concluded that it was a possibility that Pongo didn't like sharing the attention he had once enjoyed all to himself (and there were a couple of occasions with my son that supported that too, although nothing of any huge significance). He was in our lives before any of the children were born, and he was no longer a puppy anymore when my first son arrived earth side. It made sense to me that what had happened to Pongo, could have occurred to protect him, my children, and me and that had he have stuck around longer, something much worse might have taken place instead. I couldn't imagine him acting in a way that would put anyone in danger, but then again, I couldn't imagine something as awful as what ended his life happening either, so it wasn't out of the realms of possibility.

Believing that all of us were being divinely protected, even by the means of the hideous and traumatic events that had unfolded, helped me come to terms with what happened, and was possibly the beginning of me understanding my role as a facilitator in the transition of animals between this dimension and the next.

Dottie

I love big dogs, and I'd always wanted a Lurcher, so when a lady I knew told me that her Lurcher was in pup, I asked her to keep me posted. Several weeks later I got a call and the next day, we went to look at the brand-new litter.

There were five puppies in total, and I chose a little girl who was really sweet looking and seemed really gentle. It was all settled and agreed, and I said that she would be called Dottie as it suited her cute face and funny little walk.

I was so excited, and for the next few weeks I made numerous visits to my friend's house to spend time with Dottie (and all the other puppies too if I'm honest). Dottie was a really lovely little dog, and even over those few weeks, she got to know who I was and as soon as I went in, would come over to sit on my knee and play. She was scruffy with light tan, wiry fur and big dark eyes, and I couldn't wait to get her home.

The day before she was due to come home, I got a phone-call saying Dottie wasn't very well. They weren't sure what was wrong, but she was seeing the vet later that morning and my friend told me she would call as soon as they were back home. I waited anxiously for the phone to ring, and soon after, it did. I answered it, and my friend told me that Dottie had died. Her oesophagus had collapsed, and despite the best efforts of the vet, she was too poorly and had died in the examination room. I was devastated. It was so sudden, and didn't seem real. I never got to bring Dottie home, and decided there and then that I could never have another Lurcher. Dottie was just eight weeks old.

Whilst I fully acknowledge that knowing any animal for eight weeks is no-where near the same as having had them in your life for years, after what happened with Dottie, it became clear to me that any relationships we form, all start with the same intensity and amount of love. Loving something, or someone, for eight weeks is an emotional investment that no one undertakes lightly, and neither did I.

Losing Dottie wasn't as traumatic or as upsetting as losing Pongo because my life, and a large amount of memories from it, weren't padded out with her, but the amount of emotion that I invested was exactly the same. It still hurt, and it took some time to come to terms with. Again, I searched my soul for a reason why it might have happened the way it did, and the answer was surprisingly similar. Maybe Dottie wouldn't have been happy in our family, and maybe there would have been a much more difficult ending had she been able to stay. Added to that, I couldn't help but feel that there are some things that just aren't meant to be, and this must have been one of them. Losing Dottie so soon and before I even really had her, made me think about the concept of love in relation to time, and that was something I'd never even considered before. What I couldn't have known back then, was that through experiencing loss, it was something I would come to learn a lot more about.

Princess Tinkerbell Pixie Paws (Tinks for short)

I'd been thinking about getting another dog for a while, and I'd been keeping my eyes and ears open to see if a rescue came up that suited the bill. I wanted a medium sized dog, who was lively and good with children, but after weeks of looking on the relevant websites, nothing had come up. I'd registered with some rescue centres nearby, and was happy to wait until the right dog presented him or herself.

One night, at around nine o'clock, I got a weird text. It wasn't from a number I recognised, and it said that there was a dog that had been taken to a pound in a neighbouring village who would be put to sleep in the morning. No one wanted her as she had been in kennels too long, and her imminent demise was purely because she had outlived the shelf life that had been assigned to her. The unexpected message gave me a different number to call if I was interested, and told me not to wait as I would be too late.

I called the number straight away, even though it was late, and a man answered. He wasn't friendly, but told me that if I wanted to come and see her it would have to be right then. I told my then husband I had to go because I couldn't just leave her to die, and I jumped in the car without a second thought.

It was about a twenty-minute journey to the pound, and to be honest, when I arrived, I had visions of some weird thriller movie where a woman is lured to an obscure place in the middle of nowhere in the dark, and murdered! It was bleak, dark and cold. The rain was pouring down, and as I stepped into the night, the smell of wet dog and faeces filled my nose. It was an awful place. I walked towards the only building I could see, and saw a man walking towards me shining a torch on the path so we could both see it, albeit from different directions. There weren't really any pleasantries, and he ordered me to follow him to the kennels. As we turned the corner, I could see that the building was made up of concrete cells, with thick wire fronts that stood about ten foot high. The roof was just sheet metal and there were no beds or comforts inside them at all. There were at least twenty pens, all of which had a dog of some description in. The smell was overwhelming, but the noise was worse. Every dog was barking its heart out, almost screaming at me as I walked past. My heart was racing and I felt sick knowing that a place like this existed, but I kept following the man, whose name I still didn't know.

He stopped at a cage about half way down the first row and said:

"This is it."

I turned to look inside, not knowing what I was even there for, and in the darkness, I saw a jet black, scruffy looking dog sat bang in the middle of the floor, looking straight at me. I crouched down and said hello in a gentle voice, and with that she launched herself forwards onto the wire front of the pen, and started to climb! I'd never seen anything like it (I still haven't), but in the few moments that passed, as I stood completely a gasp at what she was doing, she scaled the entire ten-foot frontage and jumped off the top of it towards me. I caught her in my arms and she wagged her tail furiously as if she'd known me for years! The man with no name was as astonished as I was. He said something like "and you've never seen this dog before?" and as I replied that I hadn't, we turned and walked away from the awful and depressing container, and sadly, the nineteen or so dogs who were left in it, who I knew wouldn't see another sunrise.

That was it. It was a done deal. I gave him no money and neither did he ask for any. He wished me good luck, and walked away into the darkness the opposite way from where we had just come.

I reached into my jeans pocket for my car keys, still cradling my new addition in my arms, and tried to block out the incessant barking that was still coming from behind me. I unlocked the car and slid in to the driver's seat, putting the black, and rather smelly fluffball I'd been carrying since she did some crazy SAS escape move, onto the passenger seat next to me.

I sat and looked at her properly for the first time. She was a just a baby, no more than eighteen months old I guessed. She had shiny jet-black eyes, a lot of black fur, and looked like a small wolf. She was smiley, and she just sat there, looking back at me as if it was a perfectly normal night. I told her it was all going to be alright, and not to worry anymore, and we set off home.

I drove the journey home in a state of shock trying to process what I'd seen in the half an hour previous. I couldn't believe that places like that actually existed, and I wondered who the hell it was that had text me in the first place! How had they got my number? Who was the guy I'd just met, and what was the place I'd just been to?

The dog just sat there in the passenger seat, looking at me, or out of the front window, not moving a muscle. She was good as gold, and I was completely stunned by her incredible demeanour and good manners. Why on earth was she in a place like that?

I got her home and carried her inside via the back door to the kitchen. I put her on the kitchen table so that I could have a look at her in decent lighting, and she just sat there like it was no big deal.

Over the next couple of hours, I bathed her, brushed her, and made sure she was fed and watered. She allowed me to do it all without incident, and if you hadn't have known differently, you'd have thought that she'd have lived with us for years!

She was my dog (she followed me everywhere), and she was incredibly special, so despite the protestations of the children, I decided that I would choose her name. I think they thought I was going to call her something boring, but I'd already chosen, and they laughed like crazy when I announced that she was going to be called Princess Tinkerbell Pixie Paws.

Tink fitted into family life as if she'd never been anywhere else. I trained her to do lots of tricks (although recall was not her strongest point) and our best party trick was when I bent down slightly to clap my palms against my thighs quickly, and then stood up and opened my arms wide. That was her queue to jump up so that I could catch her, and it never failed. It reminded me of the night I first found her, and she was as quick as a little mouse every time she did it.

I took her to dog agility for a while, which she was incredible at while we were in the training barn, but get her out on an open field and you may as well piss in the wind as expect her to pay attention. She loved people, and was one of the most loving dogs I've ever known, and even after three years together, I was still no wiser as to why she had come to be in that god-awful place the night I got that text. I was meant to find her, and she was meant to find me too…it was that simple.

Tinkerbell's "finding" story is the Not Normal Thing that happened, although what came about at the end of our time together wasn't standard either I suppose. Sadly though, it happens to a lot of people.

In the midst of my first divorce, I was forced to move out of my family home with the children, and in agreeing to do that, I asked my soon to be ex-husband to keep the dogs so that me and the children could still see them. I knew I couldn't take them with me as I would have to rent a house, but I hoped that once I was settled, I would be able to bring them to live with me again even though I knew it would take a while. He agreed, and we left, moving into rented accommodation where no pets were allowed. He went back on that promise a week later, and told me in a phone call that if I didn't find a home for her (and another dog that we had, who I haven't talked about) he would take her to the RSCPA shelter. I was totally distraught. I shouted and screamed, begged, and cried a lot, but it made no difference. His mind was made up, and he gave me a week to see if I could find good homes for them.

Thankfully, I found a home for Tink with a very good friend of mine who fell in love with her the first time they met at my house the year before. I knew she would be well cared for, and happy, and that's all I could ask for at that time.

I was absolutely devastated by it. I felt as if I'd abandoned her (them) even though I had no choice. The children were destroyed by it too, and it was really hard to explain it to them and make them feel ok about it, when it wasn't ok at all. The friend who took Tink into her family was amazing and would send me photos and updates, but they were too hard to look at. It was too painful for me to see her living with another family, and that made me feel guilty too. I should have been happy that she was alright, and I was, but knowing she was happy and *seeing it* were two very different things, so I didn't look at the pictures and stayed away as much as I could.

It took me a really long time to get over that particular trauma, and it wasn't until about nine years later that I felt able to look at Tinkerbell in her happy family life without bursting into tears, but I did get there in the end. What's even better is that I've even been to see her now. She's an old lady, and it had been about ten or so years since I'd last seen her when I went on the three-hour trip to visit. I was worried that she wouldn't recognise me, but she did, and it was a really happy day knowing that she's had a full and wonderful life being loved by many, and it's of some solace to me that I gave her that chance despite also being the one who had to leave her too. Tinkerbell is about fifteen now, and is still living very happily, in Wales, with her family.

As I've said before, the emotional investment and amount of love that I had for Tink was no different than with any of the animals that I've known, but the circumstances of our meeting meant that the bond that formed as a result, was much greater. What happened between us was an incredibly difficult experience to comprehend, and the nine years it took me to be able to look at photos of her new life, were filled with the soul-searching I'd previously found to be relatively easy by comparison.

The problem was, I wanted so desperately to work out why animals would die so young, or leave so quickly after they came to me, that I couldn't see any spiritual or higher reason for any of it, and had lost sight of why I'd chosen to look after them in the first place. I was angry, but it wouldn't be until I'd experienced a few more Not Normal animal Things that I would be able to see past the anger, pain and sadness, and discover that that was exactly where the answer was hiding.

Dottie ii

About eight years ago, during the most difficult period of my life, I decided it was time to get another dog. I hadn't had one since I had to say goodbye to Tinkerbell, and felt it would be a really positive thing for me and the children, who were all desperate for a dog too. There are a lot of arguments which would support the theory that this decision was an incredibly stupid one (our financial situation at the time being only one of them) and I accept the logic of them all. But…creating a teeny flicker of light for yourself, and your children, when everything else looks and feels *completely* hopeless, and you're not quite ready to do what needs doing, looks *a lot* like taking on a new puppy, and I knew that no matter what else happened, our new family member would be showered with as much love and affection as she could handle.

I decided that I'd really like a collie. When I was a child, we had a Scots Collie called Butch. He was an amazing family dog despite not being quite so great around other dogs (that's a whole other story!) and I really loved him. On top of that, he lived to the ripe old age of eighteen, and the fact that I had some prior knowledge (limited though it was) with being around a dog of that breed for all that time growing up, cemented my choice.

It was easy enough to find collie puppies for sale, and I managed to find a litter from farm dogs who lived on the Welsh border on a working farm; it seemed like the perfect place to get one from. I contacted the owner who promptly sent lots of gorgeous photos of the eleven-puppy-strong litter! They were all beautiful, but one in particular caught my eye. She was black all over with small white markings on her chest, and lovely eyes. She wasn't as big as the others but wasn't significantly small either, and I arranged to go and see her.

It was a long journey to the farm, but it was also a hot, sunny day which made it a pleasant drive. As we got nearer, I started to get more and more excited about meeting the puppies, and couldn't stop thinking about what it would be like to have a dog of my own again. It was an amazing feeling, and I couldn't get there quick enough. Once we arrived and met the owner, she took us to the stable block where the puppies and their mum were being kept. I heard them before I saw them, and the myriad of squeaks was utterly delightful! The owner went in first telling me to follow her, which I did of course.

The sight of eleven black and white puppies all tumbling around and wagging their tiny tails was beautiful, and I was instantly in love.

The farmer blocked off a few escape routes and let them out of the stables so that I could see them outside, and within a few minutes I had puppies clambering around my ankles and pulling at my shoe laces. The small bitch I'd taken a shine too was just as gorgeous in reality as she had been in the pictures, and after an hour of the puppy fest, I paid my deposit and reluctantly said goodbye for a few weeks until she was old enough to come home.

We were all really excited the day the puppy was coming to live with us, and we piled in the car to go and bring her home. Everything went to plan, and it wasn't long until she was sat on my eldest son's knee in the front seat while we made the journey home again. Once there, we put her new pink collar on and I decided that she would be called Dottie.

It may seem strange to name a puppy with the same name as another puppy you once nearly owned, and maybe it is, but I loved it, and it suited her, so I didn't place any significance on it, and that was that.

Dottie was a lovely dog and was, as is the same for all Collies, incredibly intelligent. It wasn't long until she was doing tricks and I discovered that it was as easy for her to pick up bad habits as it was to learn new ones, so I did her basic training and taught the kids how to handle her in the same way. She was affectionate and funny, and we all loved her. It felt incredible to have a dog as part of the family again, and I was determined that nothing would go wrong this time around.

At around seven months old, Dottie's behaviour suddenly changed. She started barking a lot for no reason, and seemed manic a large proportion of the time. At first, I thought she wasn't getting enough exercise, but I was walking her for at least a couple of hours a day, and training her to keep her mind busy. She had a huge garden to play in, and the children spent a lot of time throwing balls for her too. After months of really good manners, all of a sudden, I'd find her standing on the dining room table staring at me when I entered the room. She would stand in the garden and bark over and over for seemingly no reason at all, and within the space of a couple of weeks, she had turned into a completely different dog altogether.

I couldn't work out what was going on, but I knew I had to do something, so despite not knowing how I was going to pay for it, I booked dog training for the following week. Unfortunately, we never made it that far.

One morning a few days later, at around five am, I awoke to the weirdest noise coming from the kitchen. I had no idea what it was, but it started with a loud bang and turned into chair legs scraping on the floor and something else I couldn't make out. I scrambled out of bed, threw something on, and ran to the kitchen to see what was happening. I turned the corner from the lounge, but I really wasn't prepared for what I saw.

Laying on her side, under the kitchen table with a chair on top of her, was Dottie. She was violently convulsing and foaming at the mouth. Her eyes were open and she was making a strange noise. She had lost control of her bladder, and I stood looking at her not knowing what on earth was happening, or what I should do.

I moved the chair off her, and made some more space. I stroked her head and told her it was ok (which I have learnt afterwards isn't the right thing to do, but at the time I didn't even really know what had happened let alone what was best practice). I sat on the floor next to her for the next few minutes while she continued to fit, and when she stopped, she looked up at me but stayed completely still laying on the ground, with the exception of a single wag of her tail. It was surreal and terrifying, but I was thankful that it was over for her at least, and we sat there quietly for a couple of minutes before I got up and called the emergency number for the vet.

I was told that Dottie would need to rest for the day as her body would be exhausted and she needed complete quiet. I was asked a million questions about how she presented and what happened, and finally, we were booked in to see the vet the next morning as it was safe for her to rest at home and be seen in clinic the following day.

I spent the rest of the day checking on her, making sure she was cleaned up properly, getting her back on her feet and giving her lots of fuss. It was a weird day, but I was hopeful that it was a one off as the vet had suggested it could be, and that we were over the worst. The children were worried but could see that she was alright, and we all waited to see what the vet would say the next morning.

As expected, the vet told me that Dottie had definitely had a seizure, but that it was common in puppies as a one off, especially collies, and that I wasn't to worry yet. He said to treat her as normal and keep an eye on her, and of course call back as soon as possible if it happened again. I didn't have to wait very long.

The following week, Dottie had another seizure whilst she was stood in the lounge. This time it was longer, and more severe, and although I followed the precise instructions the vet had given me in case it happened again, I was scared. I called the vet while she was still fitting, and was told to time the fits each time they happened, and to go back in to see them that day.

That week was difficult. Dottie had two more seizures before the end of it so I cancelled the dog training, and we had multiple appointments at the vets to discuss medication and treatment. Over the next month or so, Dottie's seizures got longer, and her last episode lasted for a huge seven minutes. I had been told that if a seizure lasted over ten minutes there would be permanent damage, and there would be a possibility that she may not even come out of it at all, so at seven minutes we were getting way too close to that for comfort.

After the seven-minute seizure, Dottie's behaviour got much worse and one particular day, she didn't stop barking at all. She was extremely manic and the look in her eyes was different. It was as if she wasn't really there and was instead, stuck in some permanent and unusual state. I tried to calm her but nothing worked so I made another appointment at the vets. As my twelve-year-old daughter walked into the room late in the afternoon, Dottie bared her teeth, lunged forwards and went to bite her. It was terrifying and devastating all at the same time. I felt such a range of emotions, and knew that I had to do anything I could to ease Dottie's suffering, and keep us all safe. Thankfully, my daughter wasn't hurt, but we were fortunate. I called the vets and told them I needed to go straight away rather than wait the couple of hours until the appointment we had previously arranged.

Dottie was still barking constantly. She barked all the way to the vets, and didn't stop when we were inside. The vet assessed her and told me that she had damage from her last seizure that wasn't treatable. The drugs she was on weren't helping despite us trying different combinations, and she was suffering now as well as dangerous. After a long conversation, and through my desperate tears, Dottie was put to sleep that afternoon. She was just a baby; she died at only nine months old.

My decision to have another dog hadn't been an entirely easy one after what had happened in the years before, so going through yet another sudden and very traumatic loss was...well, it was pretty shit to be honest. At first, I didn't know what to think, and became angry, but as time passed the anger faded and it became a little easier to think about.

I considered once more the concept of love in relation to time, and how having someone or something in your life for a short period doesn't automatically make them less important, or less loved. I also revisited the theory that sometimes things just happen, but that didn't cut the mustard, so I carried on searching.

When Dottie arrived, I was in a *really* bad place in my personal life and desperately needed a glimmer of hope that things would be alright; that *I could* be ok. In the eight months that Dottie was with me, I went from being too scared to breathe and not wanting to carry on, to being brave enough to bring about the change in my life that would alter its course *forever*. They say that animals come into your life to give you the medicine that you need, and Dottie definitely did that for me although I didn't feel or notice it happening at the time. She came, she helped me heal a bit, and then she left. I knew how much she had given to me, but if I was subscribing to the theory that she had been some Divine intervention to help sort me out, I couldn't ignore the guilt I then felt for being the reason that she left too. What, apart from love and affection, had I given her? Why, if she was such a force for good, couldn't she stay? The answers still weren't forthcoming back then, but as with all things that fill a place in your life and are then gone, her tragic passing opened up the space for those answers to come.

Not Normal Things #8
Loved, Lost and a Timely Tomcat'
Part 2

Three years, and two cats later…

Artemis and Luna

My phone pinged one day, and it was a message from a girl I knew who lived close by. In her message, she explained that for some time, in her Grandad's garden, there had been a feral cat. The cat had given birth to two kittens a week before but hadn't been seen since. The feral mother had left them under a bush on their own, and while the girl originally thought she'd be back, it seemed that either something had happened to her, or she had abandoned them. The girl had taken them in, but they were very weak and she didn't know what to do with them. She asked me if I could help, so I told her I would go straight over and see what I could sort out.

I took my eldest daughter with me, and when we got there, we couldn't believe our eyes. In a box, in her kitchen, were the two teeniest kittens I'd ever seen. They were riddled with fleas, their eyes were still shut but covered in gunk, and they were almost lifeless. It was heart-breaking. The girl was beside herself; she had done her best but couldn't look after them, so I said I would take care of them. We put them in the car and took them straight to the vets.

Looking at them in their little cardboard box, at death's door and almost beyond reasonable hope, a rational person might have given up on them and it wouldn't have seemed unreasonable in the slightest. But I had already decided that they would survive, and that I would do whatever it took to ensure they did, so when (after examining them) the vet told me that they were only a couple of hours from death with possible cat flu, conjunctivitis and a severe case of flea burden, I told him that it didn't matter and to give me what I needed so I could take them home. He asked me to consider the work involved in hand rearing them, and also asked me to consider the emotional upset and financial losses I would suffer when they died. I told him again that they wouldn't die, and to give me the stuff I needed. He agreed, and asked me to return in a week if they did, as I had insisted, last that long (they were his actual words) and I left the surgery with medication, milk powder and a selection of other items which all used up £300 of the very small amount of money I had in my bank account.

There was no question in my mind about any of it. I just knew they'd be ok, better than ok in fact. I knew they were meant to find me, and me them, and I knew that it would work out. I knew the money would find its way back to me somehow, and it just wasn't as important to me as trying to save them was. Irrational? Maybe. Irresponsible? Probably. But not trying to help them was never an option. I was completely enamoured with them both, and despite already having two one-year old cats at home, it never occurred to me at all that it was a bad idea. How could it be? I had to at least give them a chance. Maybe I was trying to prove something to myself, but it didn't feel that way, and the joy that they brought with them was evident… the children (particularly the girls) absolutely loved them!

The next week wasn't an easy ride, but I gave them their medication several times a day, and their eyes started to open up and heal. I'd managed to get rid of the fleas easily enough, but couldn't bath them as they were still too young, and too weak. At that early stage it was imperative that they kept warm, so I used a pashmina as a sling and strapped them to my chest. They went everywhere with me, and I syringe fed them every half an hour, day and night, until they were stronger.

They survived until their first weekly check at the vets, where after his surprise to see us, he told me that I wasn't to get excited because the odds were very much stacked against them/us. He told me stories of the team of people that work for the practice, whose sole job is to hand rear orphaned kittens and how they have been doing it for years and have never successfully saved kittens as young as mine, or kittens as poorly. He told me that I should prepare myself for their death, because it would happen soon and he didn't want me to be under the illusion that what I was doing would work, and that doing so would save me some of the pain of losing them. I told him we would see him in a week's time, collected my new stash of supplies, and left for home.

The next visit to the vets came a week later after the kittens had been walking around the room I'd created as their safe space. They had even been playing with toys. They were lively and so cute it was almost impossible to bear! We named them Luna and Artemis. Luna was a silver tabby with exquisite markings and a colour that looked like the brightest of full moons, so I named her after the divine embodiment of the Moon. Artemis was a wild haired, mischievous fluffball who loved pouncing on things, so I named her after the Goddess of the hunt, Artemis. The vet was just as surprised to see us as he was the week before, and his warnings didn't end just because the kittens were recovering well. They were still less than a month old, and I was told that it wasn't over yet. However, this time, he told me they were well enough to be discharged until they needed their jabs at eight weeks which was in another month or so's time. I told him we would see him then, and he smiled and said he hoped I was right.

A month passed, and with every day within it the kittens grew stronger, funnier, happier and more settled. They were incredible, and we were all amazed by their resilience. It was hard to imagine them not being around and as their personalities became more obvious, and their health more robust, they settled into family life just like any normal kitten would. On the day of their injections, I carried them into the vets' practice with a really big (and possibly a little smug) smile on my face. Everyone came to see them, the nurses, the vets, everyone. It was a wonderful moment and when the vet was giving them their check-ups in his room, he told me that he was astounded, and that I had done an incredible job. It was nice to finally hear him say that they were absolutely fine and to know that going against his advice that first day was the right choice. It felt good, and to my relief, it meant that I could now relax a little bit and just really enjoy having them as part of our family.

Luna and Artemis lived up to their namesakes. They were also inseparable. Luna was so beautiful that someone once rang me and offered me £500 for her, but of course I said no. Hand rearing kittens like that forms a bond that you can't explain, and there was no way I ever would have, or will, part with either of them through a choice like that.

That was four years ago now. Artemis had a brain tumour which she was treated for at a specialist veterinary centre when she was a year old. It was an incredibly worrying and emotional time, and there was a point where I wasn't sure she'd make it. Her head was shaved, and the massive amount of stitches she had was a bit if a shock, but I was so happy that she was going to be alright, and it really made me realise just how strong our bond is. The operation was huge, but thankfully, she recovered fully and relatively easily, proving what a little fighter she is. The tumour was removed, but could come back at any time, so every day I have with her is a gift I treasure despite her somewhat aloof nature and delusions of grandeur. I suppose that's what happens when you name a cat after a Goddess.

Luna was perfectly healthy, but disappeared for a while last year. We were worried sick, and looked for her in all the usual ways but with no success. I kept seeing her badly injured in my mind, but didn't know if it was my worry and over active imagination, or a vision… it's hard to distinguish between the two when you're emotionally connected in the way that I was. Then, one afternoon I got a call from the vets saying that she had been handed in by someone who found her at the side of the road. She had been hit by a car and had died on the operating theatre. I was devastated. It felt like more than just losing a cat and was difficult to accept in the beginning. It had been eight weeks since she had gone missing, and it broke my heart to think of her wandering around lost, and ultimately losing her life in such a brutal way, and going through it all alone. We all grieved for our loss, and were thankful for having had her at all, and for at least having some sort of closure, but it was hard. Luna was two years old. Artemis has never liked being with any other cat since, and I don't think that will ever change.

There are so many more tragic and love-filled tales from the animals I have had that I could recount, and all have their very own unique mark of being a little bit Not Normal, but if I told you them all this would be a very, very long chapter so I'll stop with tales from my distant, and not so distant, past.

However...

In the midst of writing this chapter, a Tomcat climbed in my kitchen window, meowing wildly. He soon got shown the door (the same window that he came in through) by one of my own cats and I thought that was that. An hour later and he was still meowing as if his life depended on it, this time from outside the window, as I had closed it to stop a repeat of his earlier antics. He looked ok, maybe a tad wiry, but nothing serious and definitely nothing to suggest he was a stray or in danger. Not long after hearing him outside, he was in the back garden, still meowing and still refusing to leave. At present, three of my four cats have descended into the garden to scope him out and see what's going on. They are all ok as long as he doesn't get too close to them, and they keep circling each other carefully. I've taken pictures and videos of him, which enabled me to see that he has a small wound on his back leg and an older scab on his nose (probably from a fight). I've posted the videos and pictures on Facebook, on my own profile and in cat groups to see if anyone has lost him. My daughter has given him water and food although he seems uninterested in it, which is a good sign. I've managed to get close enough to stroke him and have a much better look at him. He's an in-tact male, so might just be on the lookout for some hot pussy action (sorry, I couldn't resist!) but then again, he might not. In the last three weeks I've been woken up in the early hours by a cat meowing in the garden (not mine, they currently stay in at night) but haven't been able to see anything. It's possible he's been around for a while, and it just so happens its today that he's chosen to come out of the shadows; on the same day that I'm writing about sick, lost or hopeless animals finding their way into my life. The irony, and possible consequences of this, are not lost on me.

In the time that passed with of all of these animals being found, loved and lost, I didn't just come out of the spiritual closet, but came bounding out in a blaze of glory wearing bright red trousers with orange spots, a neon jumper with a giant bow, and honking a child's party blower as I landed in the room (hypothetically speaking), which *should* have made it easier, but …it most definitely did the exact opposite! Despite my overtly conscious lifestyle and ever-evolving belief systems, I still didn't understand why it seemed that animals came to me to die (that's exactly how it felt, and mostly happened) and I didn't want to carry that mantle if it was true either. But what I was sure of, was that it taught me a lot about life, death, love, loss, and also time.

By the time Artemis and Luna had come along, I'd studied a wide range of topics including symbolism, Gods and Goddesses, Shamans and the history of Shamanism, Twin Flames, Soul Mate relationships, The 3rd,4th,5th Dimensions and beyond, Witchcraft, a hundred different spiritual belief systems and healing modalities including Reiki, Shamanic Journeying, Past life Regression and *so* much more.

Reading about how Twin Flames can be animals, and you need to learn the lessons that they come to teach you, or you'll repeat them at your peril, is pretty daunting when you don't know what the lesson to be learnt is in the first place. And having a history (which by now I did) of animals dying or leaving suddenly at a young age, made that feel even worse. I started to feel that I was either a really stupid or just plain bad person who deserved what I was getting, which obviously, made trying to understand it all almost impossible.

I read a lot about taking responsibility for the events in your life that you see as bad things that happened "to you" and how you should start seeing them as things that you had a responsibility for instead, and again, I took it literally and felt a great weight on my shoulders, blaming myself for it all (and *totally* missing the point of course).

I also contemplated that maybe they find me because *they know* they're going to have a short life. It's like they somehow know I've had to develop a healthy attitude to their death (as much as anyone can at least) and that it doesn't frighten me it as it does many people. That doesn't mean I'm any less distressed when they pass, of course I am, and I feel the loss just as much as anybody, but it does mean that I come to terms with that loss fairly quickly and understand that if love is all we ever have, then no time is wasted or missed out on. With that, came more questioning about whether I am some sort of transitional gateway; like a comfortable but brief destination before you're forced to set out on the final leg of your journey. It's certainly not something I could rule out despite the uncomfortableness of the feeling it left me with.

The losses I encountered in relation to the animals I've had the pleasure of knowing (I don't like saying I own them), have been hard to bear. None more so than the sudden and traumatic loss of my horse, and an amazing and beautiful dog that came to me after that, called Mouse, who both died within a year of each other and again, at an incredibly significant time in my life. That was only three years ago in 2017, and it has occasionally weighed heavy on my mind that as long as I have animals, I am repeatedly opening myself up for this particular type of pain.

It's hard to explain how the overall aspect of it has felt at times too. I mean, to be honest, I've found it a little bit fucking embarrassing in the past. No, not embarrassing, that's the wrong word. I suppose what I mean is that sometimes I've felt ashamed of it all. I've felt ashamed that all of these animals, with all of their remarkable and often tragic stories, have been looked after by me; I'm the common denominator so what does that say? But as well as that, I've also been very aware that I've given a lot of animals a chance that they wouldn't have ordinarily had, and that can't ever be a bad thing.

As well as that, people get very upset about animals, in fact, more so than they do about people a lot of the time, so I guess it has scared me a little that people, someone, anyone, might think that I'm the one that caused any of it. I have definitely felt judged by people about some of the events that have happened and the way that things have played out, but I can't change any of it. I can't alter the facts, or the way in which things turned out, and I can't control the way that anyone else feels about it either. I've had to accept that it is the way that it is, and *that* has been really challenging.

Living a conscious life and believing in some of the ideologies that I believe in, can sometimes mean that people have certain expectations about the way you are, and how you act. I've found that when it comes to some of the awful events surrounding the animals in my life, and the way that situations have unfolded for me, has meant that I've been expected to "learn a lesson" from them. It's no secret that in every situation we experience, there is something to take away for us, and almost always we are told that if we don't learn from it that time, it will repeat itself until we do. And let's be real, I say that myself too, and I believe it to be true. So, experiencing these unusual, traumatic and very Not Normal Things, made me hyper-aware and super critical of myself for a very long time because I felt like I must be doing something "wrong".

I couldn't help but wonder what piece of the jigsaw I was missing. I thought about it over and over again, judging myself, pulling it all to pieces and desperately trying to find "the thing" that would set me free from what has, at times, seemed like some kind of cruel curse (for the record, I don't believe in curses but that's not for now).

Over the last twenty-three years, I've been through almost every emotion in regard to this topic, and none of them served me. I've felt sorry for myself, criticised myself, disliked myself, taken the blame, shifted the blame, felt guilty, felt ashamed, felt embarrassed and also felt woefully sad. From time to time I've also tried to convince myself that I've found the answer, and for a brief time felt relief or like the cat that's finally got the cream, but not one of those times did I have it figured out at all. Well, until I actually did of course.

It's been difficult to come to terms with the loss of each and every animal I've loved, as it is for anyone who goes through the same, but losing so many at such young ages and in such unusual ways, made that more challenging. And by adding the pressure on myself of finding out what the magic key is to unlock the so-called spiritual door and stop the repeating pattern, I compounded that.

In the past I've made it about all karma, judgement, all sorts of things, and there's no doubt that there were lessons about the circle, or cycle, of life that I have learnt and lived. But the one lesson that kept tugging at my skirt hems and whispering in my ear, is possibly the most simple and obvious one of all. I can't believe it took me so long to figure it out for myself but then we often have trouble seeing what is right in front of our noses, don't we?

I've always done everything in my life from a place of love. Even the shitty stuff. There has never been a time that I haven't given as much love as possible to something or someone, and I don't mean romantically speaking. When I finally unlocked who I actually was, I also discovered that no matter what else has ever come up for me, and no matter how it unfolds and evolves, the thing that underpinned all of it, was love. And of course, it still is.

These animal encounters that have filled my life so far have been some of the most traumatic experiences I've had. Not because of the severity of the details that they are comprised of, which in comparison to being abused, or being in life threatening situations are seemingly insignificant, but because within all of those experiences, and to all of those animals, I have always given as much love as I've had to give. As a result, at times, it has felt almost impossible to cope with, let alone recover from. Sometimes people have expected me not to be as upset as I have been because I "haven't had her for very long" and whilst that may be the truth, my measure of love has never, and never will be, measured by such a man-made concept like time.

Ultimately, there is nothing I could have done to stop any of them dying, and sometimes, shit happens. Sometimes, there isn't a reason for it, except that there not being a reason at all, is the concept you need to grasp. Other times there are obvious lessons like finding the strength to be brave, or keeping hope when everyone around you is losing theirs, or maybe even being steely and determined. Sometimes, woven into the fabric of what happens, are the clues of who you really are; they are strewn along the path of your journey for you to pick up should you choose to look hard enough to find them. Those clues might look like the lessons themselves: hope, bravery, steely determination, or they might look like a subconscious action that you repeat over and over without even thinking; like being a shining beacon of the kind of love that is held firm with no expectations or any commitment of time having been promised (for example). All the rest is just white noise really; the fear of judgement that makes you judge yourself and be frightened of the opinion of others, the anger, the sadness, the desperation to figure it all out…it's a means to an end, that's all. It's rooted in ego. All the lessons that are gained from the difficult stuff are great, but for me, they're not the *reason* that these animal-orientated Not Normal Things have happened to me more than most would expect. The animals I've loved, have come and gone for a much different reason than any of those.

I was chosen as their guardian, no matter how long they choose to stay, because of love. *Love* is the simplest lesson of all, and yet the most overlooked and overshadowed. *Love* overrides all of the loss and sadness and it triumphs over all of the heartache and pain too. When I look back at Pongo, both of the Dotties, Tink, Luna and all the others, I don't feel anguish, I feel pure and unconditional love. They may have left early, or suddenly, but in the end, that made space for even more love. Ultimately, *love* is all we really have; not time, or control, reasons, lessons or loss; *just untainted, unconditional love,* and if loving so much, happens to mean that I'm a gateway to facilitate an easier transition too, then so mote it be; I'll take up the gauntlet and happily carry it for as long as I'm destined to be here too.

I still have four cats who are a complete pain in the ass, but whom I love dearly. They're all girls, and two of them are from the same litter. Penny, a short haired tabby who loves her food way too much and avoids exercise at any cost, is the oldest at a robust seven. She's always been a nervy little (big) thing who doesn't like people very much at all. She adores my eldest daughter, and recently has been getting braver and actually allowing me and other members of the family stroke her, which makes me feel really happy as she's such a sweet cat. Penny still being here is a bit of a milestone, so every time she has anything minor wrong with her, there's a flicker of internal panic within me but I try to temper it as much as I can, and at the moment, she's happier than ever and perfectly healthy too.

Artemis you already know about from Part 1, but in short, she's five now and has an amazing life. She is a dirty stop out and sadly for the local wildlife, a brilliant hunter who brings all sorts of "presents" in for us; last week my daughter found a fully intact (dead) wood pigeon in her room, and on the odd occasion that one of the others attempts to kill some poor creature and doesn't manage it, it's always Artemis that finishes the job off. She loves a fuss but only on her terms, and is the only cat I know who gently (or sometimes not so gently) bites you if you stop stroking her before she's had enough. She is beautiful, and is the only one that appears to give two shits about me, so I love her a bit extra for that.

Birdy is two and is a stereotypical black Witch's cat. She has about three singular white hairs on her neck and bright green eyes and is so beautiful and elegant. She's a little bit stupid though, and whilst she has mastered the art of climbing just about anything, she has yet to do the same with getting back down again. She's noisy and meows if she's even a tiny bit hungry or decides she wants something that you're not providing. She's also very affectionate in the morning before she's had her breakfast, but if I attempt to give her a love after that, I stand absolutely no chance whatsoever. She *loves* the children though, and I mean *really* loves the children! It's lovely, and a little bit annoying too if I'm honest.

Pancake is Birdy's sister and is a tuxedo cat. She is the funniest cat I've ever known, and is utterly weird! It's the thing we all love about her most. She's tiny; much, much smaller than a normal cat, and her eyes are in a strange position on her head. They're almost too far apart and huge, which makes her look very odd. She doesn't act like a cat either. I mean, obviously she does in some ways but she's such a little weirdo and stomps around the house shouting at everyone. She likes to collect leaves, worms, feathers and twigs (I'm not joking) and brings them into the house whilst shouting loudly until she's satisfied that the entire household has heard, seen and praised her. She owns my eldest daughter and actually, if truth be known, she owns everyone else and the other cats too! She makes me laugh every day with her funny antics and if there was one cat not to mess with, it would most definitely be her. We recently found out that she may have some Siamese genes, which I've been told explains quite a lot. We call her The Alien, and as conspiracy theories go, it's quite a good one.

All of the cats are healthy and happy, although even writing that nudges me to be a little fearful again. I can see past that now though, and I have finally found peace in that no matter what happens, I know they are incredibly loved, well cared-for and bring as much joy as they are given. No amount of planning or control will change what's in store for us, so I no longer worry about it anymore; I just love them, because that's *exactly* what love itself would do.

P.S.

Life is a funny old thing. There are many things we have to have control over in order to function every-day. What time we get up, when we pay our bills, what we're having for dinner etc, etc. But we often apply the same level of manipulation to other aspects of our lives that simply don't require it, and this can not only cause confusion, but anxiety and suffering too. We get too bogged down in the detail, and if you're trying to be a conscious visitor on earth, you'll probably be desperately searching for the lessons in everything you do too.

If you look at the things that are causing you worry right now, I would hazard a guess that there are a couple that genuinely don't need to be on the list. There will definitely be at least one or two that you could easily let go of by simply relinquishing the control you're trying to have over them, and allowing them to unfold in their own time. I'm not saying you shouldn't try and find answers to the questions of your soul, but sometimes, as I mentioned before, the answers lie in the *not doing* and will come when you're ready to listen.

As I said in the pages previous to this one, I don't always have it completely figured out myself. It's important for you to understand that no one does! There isn't anyone in life who has *all* the answers all of the time; not even a tarot reading, connected-to-spirit, conscious and constant wellbeing worker-outer like me, so you definitely shouldn't expect that from yourself. But, if you stand back and examine the questions that niggle away at you, you'll often find that there is one overriding answer to all of them: love.

There is nothing that love cannot do. It can bring light where there is darkness (we all know that famous speech by MLK). It can heal rifts, bring comfort to pain, and cannot ever do any harm.

Take a look at some of the areas that cause you to feel difficult emotions, and think about whether your unrealistic expectations about being on top of everything and having all the answers, mean that you're adding to your own load.

Where can you let go a little bit, and where can you bring more love into the thing you've let go of?

Maybe something has happened to you that invokes sadness or fear. Try looking at whatever it is from a fresh perspective and search for the love that's within it. It will be there somewhere; it always is.

Maybe you need to love yourself a little more, or maybe you're not allowing love into your life for fear of being hurt again?

Is letting go of your control over certain things, a lesson that you need to learn? And if it is, why have you been trying so hard to control it in the first place? Bring some more love into that too.

Where in your life right now can you allow, or give, more love?

When you're faced with difficult questions that you don't know the answer to, ask yourself what love would do, and then *do that*. If you always work from that perspective, you can't go wrong, not in the long run.

Being more loving, allowing more love, and always taking action from a place of love *does not* mean you'll never get hurt or suffer hardships again. That's impossible, and is also part of the tapestry of life that we need to grow and learn from, but if you go into everything *from a place of love and with genuine loving intentions*, even the really difficult and not so fluffy stuff will feel easier, more resolute, and better than it otherwise would.

Like I said before, being pure love is the simplest lesson that we can learn and should be the basis for all things. Sometimes the answers for the rest of it just comes, and sometimes they take longer but arrive in the undoing. Either way, if love is at the core of all we do, time doesn't matter and everything flows better, integrates with ease, and feels much more in alignment.

My hope is that my undoing of this aspect of this Not Normal Thing gives you what you need, and I'm fortunate that in unpicking it and laying it out, I've been able to share even more love with you.

Not Normal Things #9
Going In, Instead of Going Out

In the midst of me writing Not Normal Things, a *very* Not Normal Thing is taking place. Covid-19, the global pandemic that is killing thousands of people and sending the entire world into a panicked frenzy, is an insanely Not Normal Thing, and because of it's all-inclusive nature, we are all going through it together.

As far as Not Normal Things go, it's right up there, and whilst it is affecting everyone on the planet, I can't speak for all of everyone else, so I will share part of my own story in the hope that you can take away something helpful and worthwhile from it.

From the very beginning of this weird, messed up experience, I have felt extremely conflicted. As the whole situation is still unfolding in real time, it's hard for me to work out exactly what I believe, or don't believe, and as such it's also difficult to comment on those things succinctly. I certainly don't want to get into politics either, as tempting as it might be, because that just isn't the nature of this book. There are some things I am clear about though, most of which are taken from a spiritual perspective, so I will focus on those.

I live in the UK, and way before movement restrictions were announced, it became clear very quickly that the new default position for the collective was rooted in fear. This situation was new for everyone, and none of us had a clue how to deal with it. In true human style, we started the separation process quickly by either panic buying like a mofo, or using social media to ruthlessly attack those who choose to fill any spare corner of their house with loo roll. We didn't know how long it was going to go on for. We didn't know if we would be ok. We didn't know if our loved ones would be ok either. We were worried about our jobs, money, homes being secure, and death. Nothing was the same anymore, no one knew what to expect and we had no remotely similar previous experiences to draw from. All of a sudden, we had all been thrown into the unknown and with no end in sight, it would have been easy to feel a lot like you were being thrown into a lake with bricks tied to your ankles, and many people did, but I wasn't one of them.

In the beginning of this whole thing, I just didn't feel frightened about those things. I wasn't worried about catching it, and I certainly wasn't worried about not having enough food or cleaning products either. I wasn't worried about any of the practical things at all. There was however, one fear led thought that occupied my brain over those first couple of weeks... being separated from my partner for the (potentially) three months that we might go into lockdown for.

My partner lives forty-four miles away and if we went into lockdown, would be classed as a key worker, so we knew that he would have to stay at home so he could still work, while I would have to stay an hour and a half away with my children. The thought of being without him, or not seeing him for three months, terrified me. It kept me awake at night in fact. I cried about it before it even happened, and found myself having more and more panic attacks every day that the infection got worse, and lockdown grew closer. I spoke to him about it often, and although I *knew* that we would be alright no matter what, I couldn't shake the constant fear and worry it caused me.

Then, inevitably, lockdown (if that's what you can call what happened in this country) happened. I was completely distraught. I felt like the rug had just been pulled out from under my feet. It was ridiculous for me to be so affected in the way I was, and I knew that, but I couldn't rationalise it. That day I cried a lot and felt really angry that my life had been controlled and affected in this way. It was hard to listen to people saying how it wouldn't be forever, because it already felt like a lifetime to me and at that time, it had only been a few hours. But I was also well aware that I was thinking irrationally, and that the only thing I could do, was to try and make some sense of it all.

My partner and I came up with a plan full of little things to make the separation we were forced into easier for both of us, which helped a little. But I was really struggling, and I knew this awful feeling of fear wasn't going to go away unless I worked out why it was affecting me so much in the first place. I decided that I would allow myself a couple of days grace to allow and feel it all, but that after that, I would start the work that was necessary for me to free myself from the self-imposed prison I had unwittingly put myself in.

Whilst lockdown itself has been difficult in so many ways for almost everyone, I believe that there have been some really positive things to come from it too. One of those being the chance for introspection that it has gifted people. Almost everyone I have spoken to about it has told me how they have had time to realise that certain aspects of their life needed to change because they were unhappy. More often than not, those insights have meant that people have made what were previously, scary decisions, and now have a deeper understanding about what it is that makes them feel whole. It has enabled them to create, and live, the kind of life they really want to. In some cases, including mine, it not only helped show areas that need change on a practical level, but gave me the opportunity to look deep within myself at an area that clearly needed more attention than I was giving it. I know that had lockdown not happened, I would still be carrying around the hurt pieces of myself that I was about to dive deeply into healing. To me, that is such an incredible, beautiful and powerful gift to have received, even if it has come unexpectedly, and from such an unwanted and damaging source. I'm grateful not only for the chance to do that deep-diving, but also for the almighty kick in the stomach that the sudden restrictions gave me so that I was aware I needed to do it in the first place. Like I have said before, being uncomfortable is where the biggest growth comes from, and I knew that if the amount of fear I felt was anything to go by, the freedom and growth I would be rewarded with once I'd delved into it and did what I needed to, would be incomparable, and worth every second of difficulty.

The couple of days I had allowed myself to feel angry, scared (no, not scared actually, I was petrified!) and incredibly sad had passed, and whilst I was ready to stop feeling so bloody awful and out of control, I wasn't as ready to start looking at why I was spiralling so wildly. Despite that trepidation, I knew I had to, so when I woke up one morning in the beginning of the second week, I decided that the work would start that day.

I did my usual morning meditations, had breakfast, and then sat with my eyes closed and drifted into my already rambling, difficult, emotionally charged thoughts. I had conversations in my own head and asked myself questions every time something upsetting came up. I quickly discovered similarities to events from my past, and started journaling it all. Every spare minute I had, I devoted to looking inwards. I answered the questions I didn't really want to answer. I remembered things I didn't really want to bring back into my awareness. It was exhausting; I was on an emotional rollercoaster that had more unexpected twists and turns than even I had imagined, and I had no idea when the ride would end either, but I pushed onwards. Every day I did the same; meditated and asked for guidance, drank Cacao, performed ceremony, and sat quietly immersed in music and my own thoughts. Over the space of a week, things started to feel easier. I had been shown, through my own realisations, divine imagery, and resurfacing memories of past events, why I had felt as frightened by this forced separation as I had, and it all started to fall into place.

When I look at the men I have cared for deeply in my life, there has been a common and reoccurring theme; forced separation. My Mum and Dad divorced when I was fifteen, and although I had felt emotionally separated from my Dad since he took a hairbrush to me that day in the bathroom ten years previous to that, the already present separation, became much more significant and final when he left the family home and our relationship never recovered after that. There were others too, some who I had a deep friendship with, and others who were more than that. All of them were willingly complicit in allowing my affection, be it platonic or otherwise, and all of them left. Don't get me wrong, some left just as a result of circumstance and to move on with their lives as people do, but many left as a result of treating me so badly that I was forced into separating from them. When I looked at the detail, I worked out that in every serious relationship I've ever had, I have had to end it, and be left alone, for one reason or another. That was obviously my choice, and not unusual in itself, but on closer examination of the situations surrounding those relationships, *all* of the endings that I had to

243

enforce, came about after a period of separation: moving out of the family home, a long holiday, or working away from home every week. *Every single serious relationship* I've ever had, ended as a direct result of *changes* brought about by some form of *forced separation*. Wow. No wonder I felt as scared and out of control as I did. It was a complete revelation, and one that I couldn't believe I hadn't seen before.

Nothing changed in my relationship, as there was never anything that needed *to* change, but letting go of all of that, and seeing it for what it really was (the frightened angst of a woman who was scared that forced time apart would repeat history, and bring about changes that might affect her present relationship) was liberating in more ways than one. Not only did I get to heal it all and stop carrying that particular burden around with me, but I also got the chance to fully witness the relationship that my partner and I have for the beautiful, supportive, conscious partnership that it is, *without* the fear of an unheard yet familiar voice from my past pointlessly nagging away at me in the background. *That*, is an insanely beautiful gift which has brought me more freedom than I can express. It was like having an ancient door suddenly unlocked, and with my newly felt emotional freedom, my panic attacks stopped, and I could breathe easily again.

The revelations didn't stop there either. Over time, and with everything I was working on and had built over the last few years falling away, I suddenly found myself with a lot more time on my hands. I wasn't spending hours on social media promoting my services, or doing some of the things that I thought I *should* be doing in order to make my business more "successful", and that gave me time to think about it all properly. I felt liberated, and less anxious. I soon discovered that the way that I had been working wasn't what I really wanted, and what I had initially set out to do with my work had been lost along the journey somewhere. I spent time meditating and ruminating on what it is I *really* wanted to create right *now*, and what I wanted to actually *be*, and the answers were surprising. It turned out that I had been wasting time filling my days with products or services that would do "ok" as a way of keeping myself small. I had fallen into a pattern of believing that I couldn't do what I really wanted because I'd never done it before, and had been told by others it wasn't a good idea. I kept circling round and round in the same old ways so that I didn't have to put myself out there as exactly who and what I truly am, and could avoid the fear that comes with doing just that. I was playing safe to stay comfortable even though it felt icky doing that. I decided that I would change everything that needed changing, and go back to what has always been at my core, and so I gave up any thoughts about whether it might work, or whether people would like it, and started creating from my soul. It felt breathtakingly exciting, it still does, and whereas previously I would have been checking in to ask "am I on the right path?" at every key step, there was no such question or uncertainty any more, and I don't think there will be again now. That makes it sound easier than it was though, and there was a point a few weeks in, that I considered jacking it all in and just getting some job somewhere that gave me a stable income. I told my children that I was feeling defeated, and that I was considering giving it all up, and the dismay in their faces was evident. I told them how tired I was of battling to get followers, and fighting for online space, and how I just wanted a stable life for them, and it was then that my daughter turned to me and said:

"Please don't stop"

My heart almost stopped beating, and when my other children joined in and created a chorus that said much the same, I knew I had work to do. So that's what I did, I worked. I worked at letting go of negative thoughts about my ability and worthiness. I worked at surrendering it all up to the Universe and creating from a place of purity without expectation. And soon enough, it felt easy, like it had in the very beginning, but with more excitement, knowledge, and surety. Lockdown gave me that gift too, and I'm pretty sure that if it hadn't happened, I'd still be treading water trying to make a way out of something that wasn't fully aligned with my soul's purpose, wants or needs.

I know I'm not alone in this kind of revelation either. My eldest daughter has gone diving in her own deep waters and unravelled the barriers that have crippled her self-confidence for a really long time, which has enabled her to make decisions about her future more easily, choose a career path and start living more passionately. My eldest son has spent time in introspect, learning more about himself, and has worked on the things that have kept him scared to go out and do things in the world. He's now raring to go and eager to make up for lost time! One of my close friends has looked inwards and realised that she has been keeping herself stuck through fear, and needs to move across the country to her spiritual home. She has already rented a new house and is off on a new adventure for at least a year. There are so many stories, from so many people, who have all used this time to look inwards and do the work on themselves that they needed to, in order to create a better and happier life for themselves, and that is simply astonishing.

If the Government wanted a more conscious spin on Covid-19 they could have used the slogan:

"Lockdown - giving everyone the opportunity for much needed shadow work and introspect."

Seriously though, if they had, they wouldn't have at least got something right.

Note to self; no politics. NO politics

Whilst I said that I don't want to talk about the differing theories about the pandemic and why it's happened, I can't write about it without saying something about what is by some, being called "The Great Awakening".

I'm pretty sure it started being called that off the back of the theory that Covid-19 was sent as part of the Universes plan to shake things up a bit and bring humanity into a more conscious way of being. Maybe that's true, or maybe it isn't, and it's irrelevant what I believe, but what can't be denied is the way that humanity *is* being more conscious since it all started.

You only have to look at all the acts of goodwill and friendship across the globe to see goodness in human nature (something we aren't shown a lot of usually), and it's clear to see that whole families now have clearer perspectives about what's important and what's not. People who normally travel miles and miles to work, are now asking if they can work from home three days a week permanently. People who previously worked all the hours God sends have cut their shifts down to get a better quality of life and spend time with the people they love. People are spending more time outside in nature, walking, cycling, running or just simply sitting on the grass and taking in the view, which can only serve to better their connection to Source (yes, even for those who don't have any concept of what that might be, or indeed have any kind of belief system at all). Our connection to each other may have suffered through lack of physical contact (which of course is vitally important, and has been increasingly difficult to maintain) but we have spent time on video calls, doing quizzes, talking, getting to know one another again, and I don't think that kind of connection should be as taken for granted as it has been in the past. Add to that all the inner work I have mentioned before, and all in all, it does seem as though thousands of people across the globe are becoming more aligned within themselves and within their lives, which can only mean that collectively, we *are* more "awake".

I have never thought that "The Great Awakening" meant that everyone would start seeing or hearing spirit or meditating daily (although, I wish they would), but more that there would be a large amount of people who would start living *their own lives* differently *and more consciously*, no matter what stage they were at in the beginning of the pandemic. It certainly *seems* like that has happened, and where it has, those people are existing at a higher vibrational level which in turn, raises the vibration of existence as a whole.

It is also certain that some of the more negative aspects of society are being shown in such clear ways that they can no longer be ignored or tolerated. People are seeing the media for the propaganda that it is (in the main) and some are doing their research and making their own minds up on matters of importance. High profile figures are being held accountable for their despicable actions, and we are becoming more aware of some of the shameful acts they are complicit in, or have facilitated, and want justice. Systematic racism is at the forefront of everything, and the Black Lives Matter movement is fighting hard so that we can all live equally. We are all one race regardless of colour, sex, gender, creed, religion or any other boundary that has been falsely erected by the elite or society as a whole, and more people are starting to understand that. There is so much change in the air that it's hard for those who think it's just another tin hat statement, to deny that we *are* in *some kind* of mass awakening.

There are of course, many things that are challenging, difficult and in some cases, completely devastating for people during this Not Normal Thing, but many of those are out of our individual control. The things we *can* control are made up of the more conscious and spiritual choices that we make about our every-day lives, and the people in them, and if you haven't looked inwards already, it's never too late to start.

In the last seventeen weeks there have been many lessons. Personally, I've gained a lot from the restrictions. Despite the lack of physical freedom we have all encountered, I've gained the freedom and joy that comes from releasing old and destructive patterns that you don't even know you're still holding on to, and hadn't even noticed before. I've gained more time with my children and been fortunate enough to witness their growth too. I've been shown once again that with the space that comes from old ways of being collapsing (in the case of the pandemic, specifically around work and career), there is always something more aligned, bigger and better, waiting to take its place, even if it doesn't feel like it at the time. I've gained the certainty that you feel when you are living fully in the present, and I've been reminded for the hundredth time, of the amazing feeling that comes when you let go of expectation, and truly surrender to what is. I've also been reminded that people, for the most part, want better things for each other and that love is *always* the winner. But, in my opinion, the biggest lesson is that not going out, means you are forced to go *in*, and that is a gift that always brings about more growth, wisdom and understanding than you can get from going, or being, anywhere else. It requires no train, bus or plane ticket and even though you might need to buckle your seatbelt, you don't even need to get in your car. All you need is the will and courage to step into the depths of what has been hiding within you all along. It's been a bumpy ride, and whilst being grateful to Covid-19 seems like an incredibly Not Normal Thing in itself, in respect to these matters, I can't help but feel that way.

P.S.

There is still so much of the unknown ahead of us. We don't know how long we will be affected by the rules, guidelines and effects of Covid-19, and that in itself can create a great deal of fear. I can't, quite obviously, say anything that will make that reality change, but what I can tell you is that taking advantage of this situation and using it as a catalyst for personal growth is not only sensible but it also necessary, as I truly believe it is one of the reasons you have found yourself in it.

Everything we encounter in our lives is a path to a better way of being, even those things which feel like they might end up dragging you under. In fact, more so those things than any others. This terrible, global event has happened to millions of us at the same time, but that doesn't alter my belief around what we experience, and why. For every person who has lived during this time, the way that they have experienced and felt it, will be different. Not just on a surface level, but on a deep cellular level too. It will have brought up different emotions for everyone, and each person will have dealt with and talked about those emotions and feelings in a different way; or not as the case may be. A hundred people can feel deeply saddened by something and react completely differently, and it's no different with Covid-19. Just because there are more of us going through it, it doesn't mean we are all feeling and processing our difficulties in the same manner, and equally, no one way is more right or wrong than any other.

What's important is that you start where you are and go from there. Work with the tools you have available to you right now, and don't be afraid to access the more difficult and upsetting emotions that you might feel come to the surface. No matter what has happened to you during this time, and no matter how good or bad you feel, there is *something* good to be learnt by everyone.

Early on in the crisis, I saw a lot of posts about us "all being in the same boat" and it drove me mad! I couldn't understand why anyone would lump everyone together and think for a second that we were all dealing with the same issues. On top of that, I couldn't work out why people were so quick to judge the way that others were clearly feeling and make them feel "less than", or try and shame them into believing that what they were experiencing was the same as the rest of the world. No situation was, can, or ever will be, the same for everyone involved.

I know I wasn't on my own in thinking this, as not long after, I saw a great quote which has been banded around a lot since, but I think accurately hits the nail on the head. It said:

"We *are not* all in the same boat at all. We are all navigating the same storm, but in very different boats indeed."

I don't know who said it originally, but it makes total sense, and summed up what I was feeling perfectly. Some boats are small and worn down, some are big, robust and flashy, and others aren't even boats at all but rafts, or bits of drift wood that have been salvaged in a desperate attempt to stay afloat. We *are* all in a different boat, and those boats might even change on a daily basis. No matter what boat we find ourselves in, we are all sailing the same ferocious storm, and as such, we should create more space, time and compassion for each other which will allow growth of the individual, *and* of the collective as a whole.

We all have a duty to look after society, but as with life in general, the biggest responsibility we have is to look after ourselves. Use this period to reflect inwards and heal the parts of you that have shown themselves during these challenging times. Utilise the position you are in to start creating the life you really crave from your soul, not your head, and don't let anything steer you off path. Healing fragments of yourself not only gives you more opportunity to evolve into a better version of being, but also enables you to understand why it's so important for everyone else to do the same. Once you feel it yourself, you want the same for them, and that automatically holds space for anyone around you that is waiting for the opportunity to step into the challenge. Your own growth directly affects the growth of those who choose to stay around you, and *that* is how a "Great Awakening" actually happens. Not everyone being on the same page at the same time or judging those that aren't there yet, but instead, everyone doing their best to be the best, happiest, most liberated version of themselves on whatever level they have so far reached, and not expecting anyone else to follow suit, but creating the space for them to do so if they chose to.

With or without Covid-19, we live in a world where we have no guarantees of tomorrow, and have huge uncertainties ahead of us so surely, we should strive to be our very best, today? Without any expectation, or judgement about who, what and where I am right now, that's what I'm trying to, and will always continue to do; surrender, allow, and grow into the very best version of myself, and I hope that this inspires you to do the same.

The End; What Is It?

In some of the Not Normal Things that fill these pages there are situations that many people will have experienced, like divorce, for example. The complexities and unusual aspects within my experiences fall not only in the details of my life and what it has been so far, but also in the fact that many of these Not Normal Things were happening at the same time. Autism didn't wait patiently for my divorce to be over or until I'd found my niche in life to bestow its difficulties on me, just as my spiritual capabilities didn't fall neatly into place in a quiet period having allowed depression to ease, or Covid-19 to pass. For most of my life I have felt like I'm juggling a hundred balls in the air at the same time, and at times, it has taken its toll.

There have been many times when I had no idea what was ahead of me despite desperately searching for a clue, and amongst pretty much all of it, all I really wanted was to be normal. I went through periods when I didn't want to hear the voices from spirit in my head, so I shut them out. I didn't want to have a failed relationship, so I ignored the issues and prayed they would pass. I couldn't level or explain my eccentricities, so I pretended to be someone I wasn't, thinking I would then fit in, but none of those plans ever worked out. And thank fuck they didn't.

Just like everyone else on the planet, I have known great loss and felt extreme pain at times, but no matter what I've faced, I've always had an inner force willing me forward. My ego would like to tell you that it was my tenacity and strength that did that, but my soul knows better. There was a combination of things that dragged me kicking and screaming into the next phase of my life all those times I was flailing in the dark, but without doubt, there were two that gave me the will to allow that. One is likely to be unsurprising and possibly a disappointing insight for you, but it is without question one half of the equation in the sum of all my recoveries and is of course, my children. Their voices have saved me from the depths more times I can recall, and the unconditional and all-encompassing love that they give, and allow me to bestow upon them, is glorious and uncontainable.

The other part of the equation is somewhat more fluid and open to all sorts of interpretation.

In every experience, hardship and difficulty, there has been another voice. It has no real sound and belongs to no one. It is easily missed and yet, when I hear it, it is shouting so loudly that being deaf to it seems implausible. It leaves no trace once it is quiet, but somehow, I can find it if I need to. It feels like the air on a November morning in wet fields when the mist hangs low and the Sun glows a deep amber on the horizon, and although it has no name, it feels familiar, as I've called it back a thousand times. It starts with a swirling torrent of unknown and falls easily into a whirlpool of unease that ebbs and flows in rhythm to my heartbeat. It dances around my body filling every inch of my flesh, and seduces me to follow whether I feel able to, or not. I have no choice but to surrender to its power, and once it has permission, it glows brighter than the most ferocious fire in the belly of the biggest volcano, lapping at the shores of my thoughts and burning up any hope of escape. It knows my name well and asks nothing of me except one simple, returning question...

- What is it?

- What is it I can do better?

- What is it I can become?

- What is it I can do now?

- What is it I can let go of?

- What is it that I can learn?

- What is it that needs to fall away?

What is that mysterious knowing sitting embedded in my core, waiting to be unlocked and released into the world? What is it that makes me dream bigger dreams, and believe that there is something more waiting around every corner? What is it that allows me to fill my heart, soul and life with the very magick that I've been told a million times doesn't exist by those who have never felt or seen it? What is it that enables me to grow and learn, and then grow some more? Reaching for it has saved me, and I know that it will only cease when I am no longer here in my human existence, and have left this interesting, challenging and beautiful physical dimension to hold space in the next.

It turned out that in searching for normality in all of the Not Normal Things in my life, I discovered some harsh, interesting and enlightening truths. At every level, I have lost faith myself, but never at any time have I lost faith in what is, and that is what I wish for you.

You have travelled through the pages of this book; a collection of stories from my life that were born out of my eternal answering of "what is it?", and the relentless hunt for anything remotely normal, and whilst I very much hope that there will be many things you can take away and consider for yourself, there are only two that I would ask you to always remember...

The only type of normal that matters, is your own, and what is it, for you?

Acknowledgements

I really dislike the bit in those speeches at awards ceremonies where celebrities go on and on and on thanking a long list of people that you've never heard of before and quite frankly aren't interested in, but I kind of get it now! I suppose the difference, and the one thing that makes me feel less icky about writing this, is that you can choose not to read, so if you're sticking it out until the very end, thanks! And if not, what the hell is wrong with you?! Where's your sense of completion for Goddess' sake?!

Writing this book has been more than I ever thought it would be. I mistakenly thought that writing about my own experiences would be easy and not bring me anything new, but I couldn't have been more wrong. I never stopped to consider how much healing and insight it would bring about through re-living traumatic events and delving into the depths of my soul (again). Maybe it's a good job I didn't because I might not have committed to it, but thankfully here we are, and I have some people to thank.

There are so many who have supported me on my voyage into authorhood (if that's not a word, it is now) and many have listened and encouraged me with their kind words and love in the last ten months, especially Lou-Lou, Sarah A.P., Rachel, Sarah B, Kev, Kat, Amber, Vick, Terrianne, and Gem. Thanks to my sisters, who have not only supported me but tolerated me banging on about it all for what seems like years, and not once told me to stfu! Thank you all from the bottom of my heart, and if you are one of those who has willed me on from the side-lines, I'm really very grateful.

Thank you to the friend who will remain nameless, but who believed I would do it before I really started, and through the kindness of their heart and their generous spirit, bought me a laptop so that I could get it out of my head and onto electronic paper. There are some friendships that need no banners or constant bolstering to stand the test of time, and ours is one.

To Eileen, who has been more than a friend throughout it all. The last ten years have been interesting, haven't they? And here we both still are. I am so incredibly grateful for you. Thank you. I love you.

To Sean from That Guys House; I have so much love and gratitude to give you. Thank you for always being honest, kind, encouraging and the sort of mentor that I never want to stop talking to! I can't believe we got here so quickly and I almost don't want it to be over! Shall we start another one now?!

To my small but elite editing team; Mills, Agnes, and Darce; thank you! Thank you, thank you, thank you! For helping, and for further improving my ever-evolving acceptance of constructive criticism. Big kisses, and a couple of inappropriate and overused semi-colons (please note the inclusion of that hyphen too!), from me to you. To Sarah; thank you SiStar for seeing me enough to be able to write my blurb, I'm so grateful and happy that you did.

To Vic; Thank you for tolerating my teenage outbursts and bad behaviour when you could have done the opposite. You gave me the space that I needed despite how difficult that must have been at times. Thank you for filling the gap that had always been in my life. Thank you for making Mum so happy and for being the enduring and complete love that any daughter would wish her Mum to have. I love you more than you know. Your constant support and presence has never been taken for granted, and if I chose again, I'd choose you.

To Mum; Thank you for seeing what no one else could. Thank you for giving me the gift of your love and for allowing me to be what I needed even if it wasn't what you would have chosen. Thank you for teaching me about dandelions, and black cats, and walking under ladders - those were the things I always loved hearing about most. Thank you for tolerating my bare footed and sometimes wild-child nature despite the fact that it sometimes drove you insane! Thank you for believing me all those times I came to you with weird stories, and for never telling me I was crazy. Thank you for always telling me I was good at English and how you loved my writing was when I was little; those moments breathed life into the dream that has brought about this book. Thank you for all of it, and so much more. I love you more than you will ever comprehend.

To my children; thank you for being everything during times when there was nothing else left. Thank you for looking after each other while I worked fifteen-hour days, and for keeping the house in some sort of order when I had no time or energy left to do it myself. Thank you for all the dinners you cooked while I sat on the sofa tapping away on my keyboard, and for pouring me a gin and tonic so I didn't have to interrupt my flow (that was important work you did right there!). Thank you for being yourselves, for loving me and for showing me what is possible if you truly believe. You are all the most beautiful, kind, talented and fucking amazing humans I will ever know, and I am so incredibly blessed that you chose me this time round. Don't ever stop shining fiercely bright, or loving ice cream.

To Michael; You know already, but thank you. For everything. For showing me what it's meant to be like, and for loving me just as I am. For giving me the opportunity to grow, and never giving up on us even when it wasn't easy. For always having my back and reminding me that I could do it when I didn't think I could. For holding my hand and telling me what I needed to hear, and for being the best and biggest mirror for me to look at myself in. Most of all for being you, and for allowing me to love you as I do. This particular dream of mine is now a reality, and I know that what we dream together, will follow the same path. You bring me the music that fills the spaces that words can't, and I thank the Universe daily for putting us on the path that allowed us to find each other. Now, shall we dance?

And finally, to Mor-Mor; There is too much to say and I don't know how to start, but thank you. Thank you for the friendship, the daily prods, and the laughter all those years ago. Who would have thought that the joke you made that day in 2010 would fuel the fire already within me to write a book; this book. I dedicate her to you. I want to thank you with every fibre of my being for really and truly seeing me back then. I wish I could find you, but it seems it is not meant to be. If you ever get to read this, know that with every chapter I completed, I thought about being able to tell you. Thank you, dear friend. Here's to life-changing moments in time, and to Magick!